Vegan Cookbook

2000 Days of Tasty, Simple & Quick Vegan Recipes – Includes a 30-Day Meal Plan for Balanced, Nutritious, and Flavorful Plant-Based Meals to Boost Health and Energy

Savoring Healthy Living Without Compromising Taste

Julianna Wiggins

Legal & Disclaimer

The content and information contained in this book has been compiled from reliable sources, which are accurate based on the knowledge, belief, expertise and information of the Author. The author cannot be held liable for any omissions and/or errors.

TABLE OF CONTENTS

INTRODUCTION

Dear readers,

Embarking on a healthier, more energized lifestyle doesn't have to be overwhelming. Many face the challenges of restrictive diets, conflicting nutritional advice, and finding meals that are both nutritious and delicious. **This book is your solution**, offering a seamless blend of mouthwatering flavors and balanced nutrition.

Inside, you'll find **over 100 exclusively plant-based recipes**, meticulously crafted to exclude eggs, cheese, and all gluten-containing ingredients. Each recipe is **100% vegan and gluten-free**, ensuring that every meal supports your health without compromising on taste. Whether you're new to veganism or looking to expand your culinary repertoire, these dishes are easy to prepare and designed to make your transition enjoyable and sustainable.

Guiding you through this culinary adventure is **Julianna Wiggins**, a passionate chef dedicated to healthy, balanced nutrition. With her expertise, you'll discover how to create satisfying, nutrient-rich meals that celebrate the vibrant flavors of plant-based cuisine.

Join us in embracing a lifestyle that prioritizes health, vitality, and joy. Let every recipe inspire you to live more fully, savor each bite, and enjoy the benefits of a gluten-free vegan diet. Here's to a journey filled with energy, well-being, and the delightful tastes of wholesome, plant-based meals.

Let's begin this exciting adventure together, turning each page towards a healthier, more fulfilling life.

CHAPTER 1: INTRODUCTION TO THE VEGAN DIET

Welcome to Your Gluten-Free Vegan Journey

Welcome to the start of your vibrant **gluten-free vegan journey**, where every meal is a celebration of flavor, health, and conscious living. This book is your ultimate guide to embracing a **100% plant-based, gluten-free** lifestyle that excludes eggs, cheese, and all gluten-containing ingredients, making your transition seamless and enjoyable.

Why Choose a Gluten-Free Vegan Diet?

Opting for a **gluten-free vegan diet** is a powerful step toward enhancing your health and well-being. A well-balanced vegan diet is rich in essential nutrients, boosting your energy levels, supporting a healthy weight, and reducing the risk of chronic diseases such as heart disease, type 2 diabetes, and certain cancers. By focusing on **whole, gluten-free plant-based foods**, you nourish your body while making a positive impact on the planet. This lifestyle not only benefits your health but also promotes sustainability and ethical treatment of animals.

What to Expect

Inside this cookbook, you'll find **over 100 delicious and easy-to-prepare recipes** crafted to be entirely plant-based and gluten-free. Whether you're new to veganism or looking to expand your culinary repertoire, these recipes are designed to be nutritious, flavorful, and accessible. From hearty breakfasts that kickstart your day to satisfying lunches and comforting dinners, each dish is a step toward a healthier, more energized you. The meal plans are structured to ensure balanced nutrition, making your 30-day transition smooth and sustainable.

Your Culinary Adventure

Prepare to explore a diverse range of flavors from around the world, with dishes that are both comforting and exciting. You'll discover everything from classic favorites to innovative new creations, all made with wholesome ingredients that are easy to find and prepare. Embrace the versatility of **gluten-free whole grain flours** such as quinoa flour, buckwheat flour, brown rice flour, amaranth flour, millet flour, and teff flour. These flours not only enhance the nutritional profile of your meals but also introduce unique textures and flavors, elevating your culinary experience.

A Journey Beyond Food

Your **gluten-free vegan journey** is about more than just changing what you eat—it's about adopting a lifestyle that aligns with your values of health, compassion, and sustainability. This path encourages mindfulness in all aspects of life, from the food you consume to how you interact with the world around you. By choosing a vegan and gluten-free diet, you're committing to a lifestyle that supports your well-being and contributes to a healthier planet.

Thank you for choosing this book as your companion. Together, we'll create meals that nourish your body, delight your taste buds, and inspire a life filled with energy and joy. **Let's begin this transformative adventure**, one delicious, gluten-free vegan meal at a time.

The Basics of the Gluten-Free Vegan Diet: What You Need to Know

At its core, the **gluten-free vegan diet** focuses on consuming plant-based foods while excluding all animal products and gluten. This means no meat, dairy, eggs, honey, or any products containing gluten. However, there are variations within the vegan community that reflect different preferences and dietary choices:

- **Strict Vegan Diet:** Excludes all animal products and by-products, including dairy, eggs, and honey. The focus is on whole foods like fruits, vegetables, gluten-free grains, legumes, nuts, and seeds.
- **Plant-Based Diet:** Primarily plant-based with occasional inclusion of animal products. Emphasizes whole, unprocessed plant foods but may include small amounts of animal-derived ingredients.
- **Ovo-Vegan Diet:** Includes eggs but excludes dairy and all other animal products. Ideal for those who want to keep eggs as a protein source while adhering to vegan principles.
- **Lacto-Vegan Diet:** Includes dairy products but excludes eggs and other animal products. Allows for the inclusion of items like cheese, yogurt, and milk, while avoiding meat and eggs.
- **Lacto-Ovo Vegan Diet:** Includes both dairy and eggs while excluding meat and other animal products. A more flexible approach that allows for a broader range of foods while maintaining a plant-based foundation.

Key Nutrients in a Gluten-Free Vegan Diet

Regardless of the variation you choose, it's essential to be mindful of certain nutrients to ensure a balanced and healthy diet:

- **Protein:** Incorporate plant-based sources like beans, lentils, tofu, tempeh, quinoa, and gluten-free whole grain flours. These foods are rich in protein and provide a variety of other nutrients.
- **Calcium:** Obtain calcium from fortified plant milks, tofu, leafy greens, almonds, and chia seeds to support bone health.
- **Iron:** Consume iron-rich foods such as lentils, chickpeas, spinach, quinoa, and fortified gluten-free cereals. Pair them with vitamin C-rich foods to enhance absorption.
- **Vitamin B12:** Rely on fortified foods like plant milks, nutritional yeast, and take a B12 supplement to meet your needs, as this vitamin is not naturally found in plant foods.
- **Omega-3 Fatty Acids:** Include sources like flaxseeds, chia seeds, walnuts, hemp seeds, and consider an algae-based omega-3 supplement to support heart and brain health.
- **Vitamin D:** Obtain vitamin D from fortified plant milks, sunlight exposure, and supplements if necessary.
- **Zinc:** Incorporate zinc-rich foods such as pumpkin seeds, lentils, chickpeas, tofu, and gluten-free whole grains. Soaking or sprouting legumes and grains can enhance absorption.
- **Iodine:** Ensure adequate iodine intake by using iodized salt or consuming seaweed in moderation.

Essential Gluten-Free Whole Grain Flours

To create delicious and nutritious gluten-free vegan meals, it's important to include a variety of **gluten-free whole grain flours** in your pantry:

- **Quinoa Flour:** High in protein and essential amino acids, perfect for baking and thickening sauces.
- **Buckwheat Flour:** Rich in fiber and antioxidants, ideal for pancakes, bread, and pastries.
- **Brown Rice Flour:** Versatile and mild in flavor, suitable for a wide range of baked goods and coatings.
- **Amaranth Flour:** Packed with protein and lysine, great for gluten-free bread and baking.
- **Millet Flour:** Light and slightly sweet, excellent for muffins, cakes, and flatbreads.
- **Teff Flour:** Nutrient-dense with a unique flavor, perfect for Ethiopian injera and other baked goods.

Building a Balanced Gluten-Free Vegan Plate

To ensure you're getting all the necessary nutrients, follow these guidelines when building your meals:

- **Half Your Plate:** Fill with a variety of colorful vegetables, rich in vitamins, minerals, and fiber.
- **A Quarter of Your Plate:** Include whole grains or starchy vegetables, providing sustained energy and additional nutrients.
- **A Quarter of Your Plate:** Focus on proteins from plant-based sources to keep you satisfied and nourished.

Embracing the Diversity of a Gluten-Free Vegan Diet

One of the most rewarding aspects of a **gluten-free vegan diet** is its adaptability. Whether you choose to include dairy and eggs or prefer to keep strictly plant-based, there is a world of delicious and nutritious options available. Explore different cuisines, try new ingredients, and discover how versatile vegan cooking can be. Incorporate a variety of gluten-free whole grains and flours to add diversity to your meals and keep your palate excited.

Benefits and How to Transition to a Gluten-Free Vegan Diet

As you explore the world of **gluten-free veganism**, you'll discover numerous benefits that extend beyond personal health to environmental and ethical impacts. This section delves into these advantages and provides practical tips for a smooth transition.

The Benefits of a Gluten-Free Vegan Diet

- **Improved Health and Well-Being:** A well-planned gluten-free vegan diet is rich in essential nutrients, antioxidants, and fiber, contributing to overall health. Studies show that vegans tend to have lower cholesterol levels, blood pressure, and BMI, reducing the risk of chronic diseases.
- **Weight Management:** Many find that a gluten-free vegan diet helps maintain a healthy weight without extensive calorie counting. Plant-based foods are generally lower in calories and fat but high in nutrients and fiber, keeping you full and satisfied.

- **Increased Energy Levels:** Focusing on whole, nutrient-dense foods can lead to higher energy levels and improved physical endurance. Reducing processed foods and gluten can enhance digestion and overall vitality.
- **Environmental Impact:** Producing plant-based foods typically requires fewer resources like land, water, and energy compared to animal agriculture. By choosing a gluten-free vegan diet, you reduce your carbon footprint and help preserve the planet's resources.
- **Ethical Considerations:** For many, the decision to go vegan is driven by a commitment to animal welfare. Eliminating animal products from your diet means taking a stand against practices that involve animal exploitation and suffering.
- **Culinary Creativity:** A gluten-free vegan diet encourages the exploration of new ingredients, flavors, and cooking techniques. It opens up a world of culinary possibilities, allowing you to create dishes that are both delicious and nourishing.

Common Myths and Misconceptions

Addressing common myths is crucial for embracing a **gluten-free vegan diet** with confidence:

1. **Vegans Don't Get Enough Protein:** Plant-based sources like beans, lentils, tofu, tempeh, quinoa, and gluten-free whole grain flours provide ample protein. Many vegan athletes thrive on these protein-rich foods.
2. **Vegan Diets Are Nutritionally Deficient:** A well-planned gluten-free vegan diet can meet all nutritional needs. Incorporate fortified foods and supplements, especially for Vitamin B12.
3. **Vegan Diets Are Expensive:** While specialty products can be pricey, a diet based on whole foods like grains, legumes, vegetables, and fruits is often more affordable than one centered around meat and dairy.
4. **Vegan Diets Are Boring and Restrictive:** The plant-based world is vast and varied. From creamy curries and hearty stews to vibrant salads and decadent desserts, the possibilities are endless.
5. **Vegan Diets Lack Variety:** There are thousands of edible plant species, each offering unique flavors and textures. Explore global cuisines to discover new ingredients and cooking methods.
6. **Vegan Diets Are Inconvenient:** With the growing availability of vegan-friendly restaurants and gluten-free products, maintaining a **gluten-free vegan diet** is easier than ever. Meal planning and preparation can further simplify the process.
7. **Veganism Is Just a Trend:** Veganism is rooted in ethical, environmental, and health principles with lasting relevance. Its growing popularity reflects a permanent shift towards sustainable and compassionate living.
8. **Vegans Can't Build Muscle:** Adequate protein from plant sources combined with strength training supports muscle growth and maintenance. Many vegan athletes successfully build and maintain muscle mass.
9. **Vegan Diets Are Only for Certain Demographics:** A **gluten-free vegan diet** is suitable for people of all ages and lifestyles, including athletes, professionals, students, and families.
10. **Vegan Food Is Always Healthy:** Not all vegan foods are inherently healthy. Focus on whole, minimally processed foods to ensure a nutritious diet, while enjoying vegan treats in moderation.

How to Transition Smoothly

- **Gradual Changes:** Start by incorporating more plant-based and gluten-free meals into your diet. Gradually replace animal products and gluten-containing grains with plant-based and gluten-free alternatives.
- **Educate Yourself:** Learn about essential nutrients and how to obtain them from plant-based and gluten-free sources. Understanding your nutritional needs is key to a successful transition.
- **Stock Your Pantry:** Keep a well-stocked pantry with gluten-free whole grains, legumes, nuts, seeds, and a variety of spices and herbs to make meal preparation easier.
- **Plan Your Meals:** Meal planning helps ensure balanced nutrition and reduces the stress of last-minute cooking. Use the meal plans and recipes in this book to guide your weekly menus.
- **Seek Support:** Join vegan and gluten-free communities, either online or in person, to share experiences, recipes, and tips. Support from others can make your transition smoother and more enjoyable.

Essential Foods and Nutritional Guidance for a Gluten-Free Vegan Diet

To thrive on a **gluten-free vegan diet**, it's important to stock your pantry with a variety of whole foods that provide the nutrients your body needs. Here are some essential categories to focus on:

Legumes and Beans

- **Examples:** Lentils, chickpeas, black beans, kidney beans, peas
- **Benefits:** Rich in protein, fiber, iron, and essential amino acids, legumes and beans are a cornerstone of the vegan diet. They are versatile and can be used in soups, stews, salads, and even desserts.

Whole Grains and Gluten-Free Flours

- **Examples:** Quinoa, brown rice, amaranth, millet, buckwheat, teff
- **Benefits:** Whole grains are packed with fiber, vitamins, and minerals. They provide sustained energy and are a great base for many meals, from breakfast porridges to hearty grain bowls. Incorporate **gluten-free whole grain flours** like quinoa flour, buckwheat flour, brown rice flour, amaranth flour, millet flour, and teff flour to enhance the nutritional profile and diversity of your meals.

Nuts and Seeds

- **Examples:** Almonds, walnuts, chia seeds, flaxseeds, sunflower seeds, pumpkin seeds
- **Benefits:** Nuts and seeds are excellent sources of healthy fats, protein, and essential fatty acids like omega-3s. They can be used in smoothies, salads, and baking, or enjoyed as snacks.

Fruits and Vegetables

- **Examples:** Leafy greens, berries, citrus fruits, root vegetables, cruciferous vegetables
- **Benefits:** Fruits and vegetables are the heart of a vegan diet, providing a wide range of vitamins, minerals, antioxidants, and fiber. Aim to include a variety of colors in your meals to maximize nutrient intake.

Dairy Alternatives

- **Examples:** Almond milk, soy milk, oat milk, coconut yogurt, vegan cheese
- **Benefits:** Dairy alternatives provide the creamy textures and flavors of traditional dairy while being plant-based. Many are fortified with calcium and vitamin D, making them valuable additions to your diet.

Plant-Based Proteins

- **Examples:** Tofu, tempeh, seitan, edamame, protein powders (pea, hemp, soy)
- **Benefits:** These foods are rich in protein and often provide a texture similar to meat, making them perfect for dishes like stir-fries, sandwiches, and grills.

Healthy Fats

- **Examples:** Avocados, olive oil, coconut oil, nut butters
- **Benefits:** Healthy fats are essential for nutrient absorption and overall health. Incorporate them into your diet through dressings, cooking oils, and spreads.

Herbs and Spices

- **Examples:** Basil, cilantro, turmeric, cumin, garlic, ginger, thyme
- **Benefits:** Herbs and spices not only enhance the flavor of your dishes but also offer a range of health benefits, including anti-inflammatory properties and digestive support.

Nutritional Guidance for a Gluten-Free Vegan Diet

While enjoying the variety of plant-based foods, it's important to ensure your diet is nutritionally balanced. Here's how to make sure you're getting the key nutrients your body needs:

- **Protein:** Aim to include a source of protein in every meal. Combine different plant proteins throughout the day to ensure you're getting all the essential amino acids. **Sources:** Legumes, tofu, tempeh, seitan, nuts, seeds, whole grains, and gluten-free whole grain flours.
- **Iron:** Enhance iron absorption by pairing iron-rich foods with vitamin C-rich foods, such as citrus fruits, bell peppers, and tomatoes. **Sources:** Lentils, chickpeas, spinach, quinoa, fortified gluten-free cereals.
- **Calcium:** Include a variety of calcium-rich foods and consider fortified plant milks and juices to meet your daily needs. **Sources:** Leafy greens, tofu, almonds, fortified plant milks, sesame seeds.
- **Vitamin B12:** Since B12 is not naturally found in plant foods, include fortified foods or take a B12 supplement. **Sources:** Fortified plant milks, cereals, nutritional yeast, B12 supplements.
- **Omega-3 Fatty Acids:** Include sources of ALA (alpha-linolenic acid) daily and consider an algae-based omega-3 supplement if necessary. **Sources:** Flaxseeds, chia seeds, walnuts, hemp seeds, algae oil.
- **Vitamin D:** Obtain vitamin D from sunlight, fortified foods, or supplements, depending on your dietary choices and exposure to sunlight. **Sources:** Fortified plant milks, fortified cereals, vitamin D supplements.
- **Zinc:** Incorporate a variety of zinc-rich foods and consider soaking or sprouting legumes and grains to enhance absorption. **Sources:** Pumpkin seeds, lentils, chickpeas, tofu, gluten-free whole grains.
- **Iodine:** Ensure adequate iodine intake by using iodized salt or consuming seaweed in

moderation. **Sources:** Iodized salt, seaweed, fortified foods.

Meal Planning for Balanced Nutrition

To ensure a balanced intake of all these nutrients, consider the following tips:

- **Diversify Your Plate:** Include a mix of different food groups in each meal. For example, combine a gluten-free grain, a protein source, and a variety of vegetables to create a nutritionally complete dish.
- **Incorporate Fortified Foods:** Fortified plant milks, cereals, and nutritional yeast are excellent sources of vitamins and minerals that might otherwise be lacking in a **gluten-free vegan diet**.
- **Practice Mindful Eating:** Pay attention to how your body feels and adjust your diet as needed. If you're ever unsure about your nutritional intake, consulting with a dietitian can provide personalized guidance.

Conclusion

A **gluten-free vegan diet** offers a rich variety of foods that can meet all your nutritional needs while delighting your palate. By incorporating essential gluten-free whole grain flours and a diverse range of plant-based ingredients, you can create meals that are both nutritious and delicious. Embrace the flexibility and creativity of this lifestyle, and enjoy the numerous health benefits it brings.

By adhering to these guidelines and utilizing the recipes in this cookbook, you'll embark on a fulfilling **gluten-free vegan journey** that supports your health, respects the planet, and aligns with your values. Let each meal inspire you to live more fully, savor each bite, and enjoy the benefits of a balanced, plant-based diet.

CHAPTER 2: 30-DAY MEAL PLAN

Day	Breakfast	Lunch	Snack	Dinner
1	Coconut Yogurt Parfait (p.17)	Quinoa and Black Bean Salad with Avocado (p.37)	Avocado Chocolate Mousse (p.52)	Cauliflower and Potato Curry (p.60)
2	Pumpkin Protein Pancakes (p.17)	Hearty Vegetable and Lentil Stew (p.32)	Fig and Hazelnut Bars (p.50)	Stuffed Bell Peppers (p.62)
3	Veggie-Packed Omelette (p.18)	Tuscan White Bean Soup (p.32)	Blueberry Almond Bars (p.50)	Mushroom Stroganoff (p.68)
4	Black Bean Breakfast Burrito (p.18)	Curried Cauliflower and Chickpea Stew (p.33)	Cherry Cashew Bars (p.51)	Eggplant Parmesan (p.68)
5	Sweet Potato Hash (p.19)	Butternut Squash and Chickpea Soup (p.33)	Vegan Lemon Bars (p.54)	Vegan Enchiladas (p.69)
6	Quinoa Breakfast Bowl (p.19)	Creamy Tomato Basil Soup with Orzo (p.34)	Coconut Milk Panna Cotta with Mango (p.53)	Margherita Pizza with Cashew Mozzarella (p.69)
7	Breakfast Skillet with Lentils and Vegetables (p.20)	Spiced Chickpea and Spinach Stew (p.34)	Raw Brownies with Walnuts (p.54)	Mushroom and Spinach White Pizza with Garlic Sauce (p.70)
8	Walnut and Banana Breakfast Bowl (p.20)	Hearty Vegetable and Quinoa Soup (p.35)	Coconut Almond Energy Bites (p.55)	Roasted Vegetable and Pesto Pizza (p.70)
9	Cherry Almond Quinoa (p.21)	Zucchini and White Bean Stew (p.35)	Vegan Snickerdoodles (p.59)	Cauliflower and Potato Curry (p.60)
10	Nutty Amaranth Porridge (p.21)	Smoky Eggplant and Tomato Stew (p.36)	Jalapeño Lime Hummus with Rice Crackers (p.46)	Chickpea and Pumpkin (p.60)
11	Fig and Almond Oats (p.22)	Butternut Squash and Quinoa Stew (p.36)	Avocado and Cilantro Hummus with Veggie Sticks (p.46)	Teriyaki Tofu Stir-Fry (p.61)
12	Coconut Quinoa Cereal (p.22)	Quinoa and Black Bean Salad with Avocado (p.37)	Beetroot Hummus with Multigrain Flatbread (p.47)	Sweet and Sour Vegetable Stir-Fry (p.61)
13	Mixed Grain Breakfast Bowl (p.23)	Red Lentil and Quinoa Patties (p.37)	Cumin-Spiced Falafel (p.47)	Stuffed Sweet Potatoes with Chickpeas and Tahini (p.64)
14	Pomegranate Quinoa (p.23)	Chickpea and Spinach Pilaf (p.38)	Sun-Dried Tomato and Basil Hummus with Pita Chips (p.48)	Stuffed Cabbage Rolls (p.63)
15	Maple Walnut Oatmeal (p.24)	Millet and Vegetable Bowl (p.38)	Pumpkin and Sage Hummus with Cucumber Slices (p.48)	Mushroom and Walnut Stuffed Squash (p.63)
16	Blueberry Millet Porridge (p.24)	Creamy Spinach and Mushroom Pasta (p.39)	Smoky Eggplant Baba Ganoush with Whole Wheat Pita (p.49)	Stuffed Bell Peppers (p.62)
17	Sweet Potato and Black Bean Tacos (p.25)	Avocado Basil Pesto Pasta (p.39)	Mini Bell Peppers Stuffed with Guacamole (p.49)	Mushroom and Lentil Stuffed Tomatoes (p.62)
18	Vegan Eggs Benedict (p.25)	Spaghetti with Lentil Bolognese (p.40)	Fig and Hazelnut Bars (p.50)	Stuffed Cabbage Rolls (p.63)

Day	Breakfast	Lunch	Snack	Dinner
19	Spinach and Mushroom Quiche (p.26)	Lemon Asparagus Risotto (p.40)	Blueberry Almond Bars (p.50)	Mushroom and Walnut Stuffed Squash (p.63)
20	Stuffed Portobello Mushrooms (p.26)	Butternut Squash and Sage Risotto (p.41)	Cherry Cashew Bars (p.51)	Stuffed Sweet Potatoes with Chickpeas and Tahini (p.64)
21	Pancakes with Almond Butter and Bananas (p.27)	Spinach and Artichoke Risotto (p.41)	Cranberry Pistachio Bars (p.51)	Cauliflower and Potato Curry (p.60)
22	Eggplant and Tomato Shakshuka (p.27)	Sweet Potato Shepherd's Pie (p.42)	Avocado and Cilantro Hummus with Veggie Sticks (p.46)	Chickpea and Pumpkin (p.60)
23	Cinnamon Apple Waffles (p.28)	Broccoli and Rice Casserole (p.42)	Beetroot Hummus with Multigrain Flatbread (p.47)	Teriyaki Tofu Stir-Fry (p.61)
24	Breakfast Pot Pie (p.28)	Eggplant and Lentil Moussaka (p.43)	Cumin-Spiced Falafel (p.47)	Sweet and Sour Vegetable Stir-Fry (p.61)
25	Blueberry Spinach Smoothie (p.29)	Spinach and Mushroom Lasagna (p.43)	Sun-Dried Tomato and Basil Hummus with Pita Chips (p.48)	Stuffed Sweet Potatoes with Chickpeas and Tahini (p.64)
26	Carrot Ginger Juice (p.29)	Black Bean Burger with Avocado (p.44)	Pumpkin and Sage Hummus with Cucumber Slices (p.48)	Mushroom Stroganoff (p.68)
27	Cucumber Mint Smoothie (p.30)	Hummus and Veggie Pita (p.44)	Smoky Eggplant Baba Ganoush with Whole Wheat Pita (p.49)	Eggplant Parmesan (p.68)
28	Strawberry Basil Smoothie (p.30)	Portobello Mushroom Burger (p.45)	Mini Bell Peppers Stuffed with Guacamole (p.49)	Vegan Enchiladas (p.69)
29	Watermelon Mint Juice (p.31)	Zucchini and Corn Pita (p.45)	Fig and Hazelnut Bars (p.50)	Margherita Pizza with Cashew Mozzarella (p.69)
30	Tropical Sunrise Smoothie (p.31)	Creamy Spinach and Mushroom Pasta (p.39)	Blueberry Almond Bars (p.50)	Roasted Vegetable and Pesto Pizza (p.70)

Note: Please keep in mind that the 30-Day Meal Plan provided in this book is meant to serve as a helpful guide and source of inspiration. The caloric values of the recipes are approximate and may vary depending on portion sizes and the specific ingredients you use. Our meal plan is carefully crafted to offer a diverse and balanced menu, rich in proteins, healthy fats, and carbohydrates, allowing you to enjoy nutritious meals without compromising on flavor.

If you find that the calorie content of the recipes does not perfectly match your personal needs or goals, don't hesitate to adjust the portion sizes. You can increase or decrease the quantities to ensure that the meal plan fits your individual dietary preferences and objectives. Feel free to be creative and adapt each dish to suit your unique requirements. Enjoy every meal and make it your own!

CHAPTER 3: BREAKFASTS:
Quick and Nutritious Protein Breakfasts

Coconut Yogurt Parfait

Prep: 5 minutes | Serves: 2

Ingredients:

- 2 cups coconut yogurt (480g)
- 1 cup certified gluten-free vegan granola (120g)
- 1 tbsp low carb sweetener (optional) (15g)
- 2 cups mixed fresh fruit (300g)

Instructions:

1. In two glasses, layer 1/4 cup gluten-free granola, 1/2 cup coconut yogurt, and 1/4 cup fresh fruit.
2. Repeat the layers, finishing with a layer of fresh fruit on top.
3. If desired, drizzle with low carb sweetener.
4. Serve immediately.

Nutritional Facts (Per Serving): Calories: 400 | Carbs: 55g | Protein: 6g | Fat: 18g | Fiber: 8g | Sodium: 100mg | Sugars: 22g

Pumpkin Protein Pancakes

Prep: 10 minutes | Cook: 15 minutes | Serves: 2

Ingredients:

- 1 cup pumpkin puree (240g)
- 1 cup gluten-free vegan protein powder (ensure it's plant-based, such as pea or soy protein) (120g)
- 1 tsp cinnamon (2g)
- 1 tbsp olive oil (15ml) for cooking
- 1 cup almond milk (240ml)

Instructions:

1. In a bowl, mix pumpkin puree, gluten-free vegan protein powder, almond milk, and cinnamon until smooth.
2. Heat olive oil in a non-stick pan over medium heat.
3. Pour 1/4 cup of the batter for each pancake onto the pan.
4. Cook until bubbles form on the surface, then flip and cook until golden brown on both sides.
5. Serve warm.

Nutritional Facts (Per Serving): Calories: 400 | Carbs: 55g | Protein: 20g | Fat: 12g | Fiber: 7g | Sodium: 400mg | Sugars: 10g

Veggie-Packed Omelette

Prep: 10 minutes | Cook: 10 minutes | Serves: 2

Ingredients:

- 1 cup certified gluten-free chickpea flour (120g)
- 1 1/4 cups water (300ml)
- 1/2 tsp salt (3g)
- 1/2 tsp turmeric (2g)
- 1 cup mushrooms, sliced (90g)
- 1 cup fresh spinach, chopped (30g)
- 1 cup cherry tomatoes, halved (150g)
- 1 tbsp olive oil (15ml)

Instructions:

1. In a bowl, whisk chickpea flour, water, salt, and turmeric until smooth.
2. Heat olive oil in a non-stick pan over medium heat.
3. Add mushrooms and sauté until soft, then add spinach and tomatoes. Cook until spinach is wilted. Remove vegetables and set aside.
4. Pour half of the chickpea batter into the pan, spreading evenly. Cook for 2-3 minutes until bubbles form and edges start to lift.
5. Add half the cooked vegetables on one side of the omelette, then fold the other side over to cover. Cook for another minute.
6. Repeat with the remaining batter and vegetables.

Nutritional Facts (Per Serving): Calories: 400 | Carbs: 50g | Protein: 18g | Fat: 14g | Fiber: 12g | Sodium: 400mg | Sugars: 8g

Black Bean Breakfast Burrito

Prep: 10 minutes | Cook: 5 minutes | Serves: 2

Ingredients:

- 1 can black beans, drained and rinsed (15 oz / 400g)
- 1/2 cup salsa (120g)
- 1 avocado, sliced (150g)
- 2 gluten-free tortillas (200g) (Use certified gluten-free corn or flour tortillas)
- 1 tbsp olive oil (15ml)

Instructions:

1. Heat olive oil in a pan over medium heat.
2. Add black beans and salsa to the pan. Cook until warmed through, about 2-3 minutes.
3. Lay gluten-free tortillas flat and divide the bean mixture between them.
4. Top with avocado slices.
5. Roll up the tortillas, tucking in the sides as you go. Serve warm

Nutritional Facts (Per Serving): Calories: 400 | Carbs: 55g | Protein: 11g | Fat: 16g | Fiber: 16g | Sodium: 400mg | Sugars: 4g

Sweet Potato Hash

Prep: 10 minutes | Cook: 15 minutes | Serves: 2

Ingredients:

- 2 cups sweet potatoes, diced (300g)
- 1 can black beans, drained and rinsed (15 oz / 400g)
- 2 cups kale, chopped (60g)
- 1 tbsp olive oil (15ml)
- 1/2 tsp salt (3g)
- 1/2 tsp black pepper (2g)

Instructions:

1. Heat olive oil in a large pan over medium heat.
2. Add sweet potatoes and cook until tender, about 10 minutes.
3. Add black beans and kale, cooking until kale is wilted, about 5 minutes.
4. Season with salt and black pepper.
5. Serve hot.

Nutritional Facts (Per Serving): Calories: 400 | Carbs: 70g | Protein: 14g | Fat: 10g | Fiber: 15g | Sodium: 400mg | Sugars: 9g

Quinoa Breakfast Bowl

Prep: 5 minutes | Cook: 15 minutes | Serves: 2

Ingredients:

- 1 cup cooked quinoa (185g)
- 1 cup almond milk (240ml)
- 1 cup fresh berries (150g)
- 2 tbsp chia seeds (30g)
- 1 tbsp low carb sweetener (optional) (15g)

Instructions:

1. In a pot, combine cooked quinoa and almond milk. Heat over medium heat until warm.
2. Divide quinoa mixture between two bowls.
3. Top each bowl with fresh berries and chia seeds.
4. If desired, drizzle with low carb sweetener.
5. Serve warm.

Nutritional Facts (Per Serving): Calories: 400 | Carbs: 60g | Protein: 12g | Fat: 12g | Fiber: 10g | Sodium: 50mg | Sugars: 15g

Breakfast Skillet with Lentils and Vegetables

Prep: 10 minutes | Cook: 20 minutes | Serves: 2

Ingredients:

- 1 cup cooked lentils (200g)
- 1 cup bell peppers, diced (150g)
- 1 cup zucchini, diced (150g)
- 1 cup cherry tomatoes, halved (150g)
- 1/2 cup red onion, chopped (75g)
- 1 tbsp olive oil (15ml)
- 1 tsp smoked paprika (2g)
- 1/2 tsp salt (3g)
- 1/2 tsp black pepper (2g)

Instructions:

1. Heat olive oil in a skillet over medium heat.
2. Add red onion and bell peppers, sauté for 5 minutes until softened.
3. Add zucchini and cherry tomatoes, cook for another 5 minutes.
4. Stir in cooked lentils, smoked paprika, salt, and black pepper. Cook for 5 more minutes.
5. Serve warm.

Nutritional Facts (Per Serving): Calories: 400 | Carbs: 60g | Protein: 20g | Fat: 12g | Fiber: 18g | Sodium: 400mg | Sugars: 12g

Walnut and Banana Breakfast Bowl

Prep: 5 minutes | Cook: 10 minutes | Serves: 2

Ingredients:

- 1 cup certified gluten-free rolled oats (90g)
- 2 bananas, sliced (240g)
- 1/4 cup walnuts, chopped (30g)
- 2 tbsp maple syrup (30ml)
- 1/2 tsp cinnamon (2g)
- 2 cups water (480ml)

Instructions:

1. In a pot, bring water to a boil. Add gluten-free rolled oats and reduce heat to a simmer. Cook for 5-7 minutes until thickened.
2. Divide cooked oats between two bowls.
3. Top each bowl with sliced bananas, walnuts, and a drizzle of maple syrup.
4. Sprinkle with cinnamon.
5. Serve warm.

Nutritional Facts (Per Serving): Calories: 400 | Carbs: 70g | Protein: 8g | Fat: 14g | Fiber: 8g | Sodium: 20mg | Sugars: 20g

CHAPTER 4: BREAKFASTS: Whole Grain Cereal Dishes

Cherry Almond Quinoa

Prep: 10 minutes | Cook: 30 minutes | Serves: 2

Ingredients:

- 1 cup quinoa (200g) (Ensure it's rinsed thoroughly)
- 2 cups water (480ml)
- 1/2 cup dried cherries (75g)
- 1/4 cup sliced almonds (30g)
- 1 tbsp low carb sweetener (15g)
- 1/2 tsp vanilla extract (2ml)
- 1/2 tsp salt (3g)

Instructions:

1. In a pot, bring water to a boil. Add quinoa and salt, reduce heat to a simmer. Cook for 20 minutes until tender.
2. Stir in dried cherries, sliced almonds, sweetener, and vanilla extract.
3. Cook for an additional 5 minutes.
4. Serve warm.

Nutritional Facts (Per Serving): Calories: 400 | Carbs: 72g | Protein: 12g | Fat: 10g | Fiber: 10g | Sodium: 300mg | Sugars: 16g

Nutty Amaranth Porridge

Prep: 5 minutes | Cook: 25 minutes | Serves: 2

Ingredients:

- 1/2 cup amaranth (95g)
- 2 cups almond milk (480ml)
- 1/4 cup chopped nuts (30g)
- 1/2 tsp cinnamon (2g)
- 1 tbsp low carb sweetener (15g)
- 1/4 tsp salt (1g)

Instructions:

1. In a saucepan, combine amaranth, almond milk, cinnamon, and salt. Bring to a boil.
2. Reduce heat and simmer, stirring occasionally, until the amaranth is tender and the mixture is thickened, about 20-25 minutes.
3. Stir in the chopped nuts and sweetener.
4. Serve warm.

Nutritional Facts (Per Serving): Calories: 400 | Carbs: 55g | Protein: 12g | Fat: 14g | Fiber: 7g | Sodium: 250mg | Sugars: 5g

Fig and Almond Oats

Prep: 5 minutes | Cook: 10 minutes | Serves: 2

Ingredients:

- 1 cup certified gluten-free rolled oats (90g)
- 2 cups water (480ml)
- 1/2 cup dried figs, chopped (75g)
- 1/4 cup almond slices (30g)
- 1 tbsp low carb sweetener (15g)
- 1/2 tsp vanilla extract (2ml)
- 1/4 tsp salt (1g)

Instructions:

1. In a saucepan, bring water to a boil. Add gluten-free rolled oats and salt, reduce heat to a simmer. Cook for 5 minutes.
2. Stir in chopped figs, almond slices, sweetener, and vanilla extract. Cook for another 5 minutes.
3. Serve warm.

Nutritional Facts (Per Serving): Calories: 400 | Carbs: 72g | Protein: 10g | Fat: 10g | Fiber: 10g | Sodium: 200mg | Sugars: 20g

Coconut Quinoa Cereal

Prep: 5 minutes | Cook: 15 minutes | Serves: 2

Ingredients:

- 1/2 cup quinoa (85g)
- 1 cup coconut milk (240ml)
- 1/2 cup water (120ml)
- 1/4 cup shredded coconut (20g)
- 1 tbsp low carb sweetener (15g)
- 1/2 tsp vanilla extract (2ml)
- 1/4 tsp salt (1g)

Instructions:

1. In a saucepan, combine quinoa, coconut milk, water, and salt. Bring to a boil.
2. Reduce heat and simmer, covered, for 15 minutes or until quinoa is tender and liquid is absorbed.
3. Stir in shredded coconut, sweetener, and vanilla extract.
4. Serve warm.

Nutritional Facts (Per Serving): Calories: 400 | Carbs: 55g | Protein: 10g | Fat: 18g | Fiber: 7g | Sodium: 150mg | Sugars: 8g

Mixed Grain Breakfast Bowl

Prep: 10 minutes | Cook: 20 minutes | Serves: 2

Ingredients:

- 1/4 cup quinoa (45g)
- 1/4 cup millet (45g)
- 1/4 cup amaranth (45g)
- 2 cups water (480ml)
- 1/2 tsp cinnamon (2g)
- 1/4 cup dried cranberries (30g)
- 1 tbsp low carb sweetener (15g)
- 1/4 tsp salt (1g)

Instructions:

1. Rinse quinoa, millet, and amaranth under cold water.
2. In a saucepan, combine grains, water, cinnamon, and salt. Bring to a boil.
3. Reduce heat to low, cover, and simmer for 20 minutes or until grains are tender and water is absorbed.
4. Stir in dried cranberries and sweetener.
5. Serve warm.

Nutritional Facts (Per Serving): Calories: 400 | Carbs: 75g | Protein: 10g | Fat: 5g | Fiber: 8g | Sodium: 250mg | Sugars: 15g

Pomegranate Quinoa

Prep: 10 minutes | Cook: 25 minutes | Serves: 2

Ingredients:

- 1/2 cup quinoa (100g) (Ensure it's rinsed thoroughly)
- 1 cup almond milk (240ml)
- 1/2 cup water (120ml)
- 1/2 cup pomegranate seeds (80g)
- 1 tbsp low carb sweetener (15g)
- 1/2 tsp vanilla extract (2ml)
- 1/4 tsp salt (1g)

Instructions:

1. Rinse quinoa under cold water.
2. In a saucepan, combine quinoa, almond milk, water, and salt. Bring to a boil.
3. Reduce heat to low, cover, and simmer for 20 minutes or until quinoa is tender.
4. Stir in pomegranate seeds, sweetener, and vanilla extract.
5. Serve warm.

Nutritional Facts (Per Serving): Calories: 400 | Carbs: 68g | Protein: 10g | Fat: 10g | Fiber: 8g | Sodium: 200mg | Sugars: 15g

Maple Walnut Oatmeal

Prep: 5 minutes | Cook: 10 minutes | Serves: 2

Ingredients:

- 1 cup certified gluten-free rolled oats (90g)
- 2 cups water (480ml)
- 1/4 cup chopped walnuts (30g)
- 2 tbsp maple syrup (30ml)
- 1/2 tsp cinnamon (2g)
- 1/4 tsp salt (1g)

Instructions:

1. In a saucepan, bring water to a boil. Add gluten-free rolled oats and salt, reduce heat to a simmer. Cook for 5-7 minutes.
2. Stir in chopped walnuts and cinnamon. Cook for another 2-3 minutes.
3. Divide oats between two bowls and drizzle each with 1 tbsp of maple syrup.
4. Serve warm.

Nutritional Facts (Per Serving): Calories: 400 | Carbs: 60g | Protein: 8g | Fat: 14g | Fiber: 6g | Sodium: 150mg | Sugars: 15g

Blueberry Millet Porridge

Prep: 5 minutes | Cook: 25 minutes | Serves: 2

Ingredients:

- 1/2 cup millet (90g)
- 2 cups almond milk (480ml)
- 1 cup fresh blueberries (150g)
- 1 tbsp low carb sweetener (15g)
- 1/2 tsp cinnamon (2g)
- 1/4 tsp salt (1g)

Instructions:

1. Rinse millet under cold water.
2. In a saucepan, combine millet, almond milk, cinnamon, and salt. Bring to a boil.
3. Reduce heat and simmer, stirring occasionally, until millet is tender and mixture is thickened, about 20-25 minutes.
4. Stir in blueberries and sweetener.
5. Serve warm.

Nutritional Facts (Per Serving): Calories: 400 | Carbs: 68g | Protein: 10g | Fat: 10g | Fiber: 8g | Sodium: 200mg | Sugars: 15g

CHAPTER 5: BREAKFASTS: Weekend Brunch Ideas

Sweet Potato and Black Bean Tacos

Prep: 10 minutes | Cook: 30 minutes | Serves: 2

Ingredients:

- 1 medium sweet potato, diced (200g)
- 1 tbsp olive oil (15ml)
- 1/2 tsp cumin (2g)
- 1/2 tsp chili powder (2g)
- 1/4 tsp salt (1g)
- 1/2 avocado, sliced (75g)
- 1 cup black beans, drained and rinsed (150g)
- 4 gluten-free tortillas (200g) (Use certified gluten-free corn or flour tortillas))
- 1/4 cup salsa (60g)

Instructions:

1. Preheat oven to 400°F (200°C).
2. Toss diced sweet potato with olive oil, cumin, chili powder, and salt. Spread on a baking sheet and roast for 25 minutes until tender.
3. Warm black beans in a small saucepan over medium heat.
4. Divide roasted sweet potatoes and black beans between tortillas. Top with avocado slices, salsa.

Nutritional Facts (Per Serving): Calories: 400 | Carbs: 60g | Protein: 10g | Fat: 14g | Fiber: 12g | Sodium: 400mg | Sugars: 6g

Vegan Eggs Benedict

Prep: 15 minutes | Cook: 15 minutes | Serves: 2

Ingredients:

- 1 block tofu or 1 cup certified gluten-free chickpea flour (200g)
- 1/2 cup water (120ml, if using chickpea flour)
- 1 tbsp nutritional yeast (15g)
- 1/2 tsp turmeric (2g)
- 1/4 tsp salt (1g)
- 2 gluten-free English muffins, halved (200g)
- 1 cup spinach, sautéed (30g)
- 1/2 cup vegan hollandaise sauce (120ml)

Instructions:

1. If using tofu, slice into 4 pieces. If using chickpea flour, mix with water, nutritional yeast, turmeric, and salt to form a batter.
2. Cook tofu or chickpea batter in a non-stick pan over medium heat until golden on both sides.
3. Toast gluten-free English muffin halves.
4. Top each muffin half with sautéed spinach and tofu or chickpea "egg".
5. Drizzle with vegan hollandaise sauce.

Nutritional Facts (Per Serving): Calories: 400 | Carbs: 50g | Protein: 15g | Fat: 14g | Fiber: 8g | Sodium: 400mg | Sugars: 4g

Spinach and Mushroom Quiche

Prep: 15 minutes | Cook: 35 minutes | Serves: 2

Ingredients:

- 1 cup certified gluten-free whole grain flour blend (120g) (e.g., buckwheat, quinoa flour)
- 1/2 cup cold water (120ml)
- 1/4 cup olive oil (60ml)
- 1 cup fresh spinach, chopped (30g)
- 1 cup mushrooms, sliced (90g)
- 1 cup silken tofu (250g)
- 1/4 cup nutritional yeast (30g)
- 1/2 tsp salt (3g)
- 1/2 tsp turmeric (2g)
- 1/4 tsp black salt (kala namak, for eggy flavor) (1g)

Instructions:

1. Preheat the oven to 375°F (190°C).
2. In a bowl, mix gluten-free whole grain flour blend, cold water, and olive oil to form a dough. Press into a pie dish lined with parchment paper.
3. Sauté spinach and mushrooms until tender.
4. Blend silken tofu, nutritional yeast, salt, turmeric, and black salt until smooth.
5. Mix in sautéed spinach and mushrooms, then pour into the crust.
6. Bake for 35 minutes until set. Serve warm.

Nutritional Facts (Per Serving): Calories: 400 | Carbs: 45g | Protein: 15g | Fat: 20g | Fiber: 7g | Sodium: 400mg | Sugars: 3g

Stuffed Portobello Mushrooms

Prep: 10 minutes | Cook: 20 minutes | Serves: 2

Ingredients:

- 4 large portobello mushrooms (400g)
- 1 cup cooked quinoa (185g)
- 1 cup fresh spinach, chopped (30g)
- 1/4 cup sun-dried tomatoes, chopped (30g)
- 2 tbsp olive oil (30ml)
- 1/2 tsp garlic powder (2g)
- 1/2 tsp salt (3g)
- 1/4 tsp black pepper (1g)

Instructions:

1. Preheat the oven to 400°F (200°C).
2. Remove stems from portobello mushrooms and brush caps with olive oil.
3. In a bowl, mix cooked quinoa, spinach, sun-dried tomatoes, garlic powder, salt, and black pepper.
4. Stuff the mushroom caps with the quinoa mixture.
5. Bake for 20 minutes until mushrooms are tender.
6. Serve warm.

Nutritional Facts (Per Serving): Calories: 400 | Carbs: 50g | Protein: 12g | Fat: 18g | Fiber: 9g | Sodium: 400mg | Sugars: 8g

Pancakes with Almond Butter and Bananas

Prep: 10 minutes | Cook: 15 minutes | Serves: 2

Ingredients:

- 1 cup certified gluten-free whole grain flour (120g)
- 1 tbsp baking powder (15g) (Ensure it's gluten-free)
- 1 cup almond milk (240ml)
- 1 tbsp low carb sweetener (15g)
- 1 tsp vanilla extract (5ml)
- 1/4 cup almond butter (60g)
- 2 bananas, sliced (240g)
- 1 tbsp olive oil (15ml) for cooking

Instructions:

1. In a bowl, mix gluten-free whole grain flour, baking powder, almond milk, sweetener, and vanilla extract to form a batter.
2. Heat olive oil in a non-stick pan over medium heat.
3. Pour 1/4 cup of batter for each pancake onto the pan.
4. Cook until bubbles form on the surface, then flip and cook until golden brown on both sides.
5. Top pancakes with almond butter and sliced bananas.
6. Serve warm.

Nutritional Facts (Per Serving): Calories: 400 | Carbs: 60g | Protein: 10g | Fat: 14g | Fiber: 8g | Sodium: 300mg | Sugars: 12g

Eggplant and Tomato Shakshuka

Prep: 10 minutes | Cook: 25 minutes | Serves: 2

Ingredients:

- 1 medium eggplant, diced (200g)
- 1 can diced tomatoes (14.5 oz / 400g)
- 1 small onion, chopped (70g)
- 1 red bell pepper, chopped (150g)
- 2 cloves garlic, minced (6g)
- 1 tbsp olive oil (15ml)
- 1 tsp ground cumin (2g)
- 1 tsp paprika (2g)
- 1/2 tsp salt (3g)
- 1/4 tsp black pepper (1g)

Instructions:

1. Heat olive oil in a large skillet over medium heat.
2. Add onion, bell pepper, and garlic; sauté for 5 minutes until softened.
3. Add eggplant and cook for another 5 minutes.
4. Stir in diced tomatoes, cumin, paprika, salt, and black pepper.
5. Simmer for 15 minutes until the eggplant is tender and the sauce thickens.
6. Serve warm.

Nutritional Facts (Per Serving): Calories: 400 | Carbs: 60g | Protein: 8g | Fat: 18g | Fiber: 12g | Sodium: 400mg | Sugars: 20g

Cinnamon Apple Waffles

Prep: 10 minutes | Cook: 15 minutes | Serves: 2

Ingredients:

- 1 cup certified gluten-free whole grain flour(120g)
- 1 tbsp baking powder (15g)
- 1 cup almond milk (240ml)
- 1 tbsp low carb sweetener (15g)
- 1 tsp vanilla extract (5ml)
- 2 apples, sliced (300g)
- 1 tsp ground cinnamon (2g)
- 1 tbsp maple syrup (15ml)
- 1 tbsp olive oil (15ml) for cooking

Instructions:

1. In a bowl, mix gluten-free whole grain flour, baking powder, almond milk, sweetener, and vanilla extract to form a batter.
2. Heat olive oil in a waffle iron according to the manufacturer's instructions.
3. Pour batter into the waffle iron and cook until golden brown.
4. In a separate pan, sauté apple slices with cinnamon until tender.
5. Top waffles with cinnamon apples and drizzle with maple syrup.
6. Serve warm.

Nutritional Facts (Per Serving): Calories: 400 | Carbs: 70g | Protein: 8g | Fat: 12g | Fiber: 10g | Sodium: 300mg | Sugars: 25g

Breakfast Pot Pie

Prep: 15 minutes | Cook: 35 minutes | Serves: 2

Ingredients:

- 1 cup gluten-free whole grain flour (120g)
- 1/2 cup cold water (120ml)
- 1/4 cup olive oil (60ml)
- 1 cup potatoes, diced (150g)
- 1 cup carrots, diced (120g)
- 1 cup peas (150g)
- 1 small onion, chopped (70g)
- 1 cup vegetable broth (240ml)
- 2 tbsp nutritional yeast (30g)
- 1 tbsp low carb sweetener (15g)
- 1/2 tsp salt (3g)
- 1/2 tsp black pepper (2g)
- 1 tbsp olive oil (15ml)

Instructions:

1. Preheat oven to 375°F (190°C).
2. In a bowl, mix whole grain flour, cold water, and olive oil to form a dough. Press into a pie dish.
3. Heat olive oil in a large pan over medium heat. Add onion, potatoes, and carrots; sauté for 10 minutes.
4. Stir in peas, vegetable broth, nutritional yeast, sweetener, salt, and black pepper. Cook for 5 minutes.
5. Pour vegetable mixture into the pie crust and cover with remaining dough.
6. Bake for 35 minutes until crust is golden brown.

Nutritional Facts (Per Serving): Calories: 400 | Carbs: 60g | Protein: 10g | Fat: 14g | Fiber: 10g | Sodium: 400mg | Sugars: 8g

CHAPTER 6: BREAKFASTS:
Smoothies and Juices to Start Your Day

Blueberry Spinach Smoothie

Prep: 5 minutes | Serves: 2

Ingredients:

- 1 cup blueberries (150g)
- 1 cup fresh spinach (30g)
- 1 banana (120g)
- 1 cup almond milk (240ml)

Instructions:

1. Place all ingredients in a blender.
2. Blend until smooth.
3. Serve immediately.

Nutritional Facts (Per Serving): Calories: 200 | Carbs: 40g | Protein: 3g | Fat: 3g | Fiber: 5g | Sodium: 100mg | Sugars: 25g

Carrot Ginger Juice

Prep: 10 minutes | Serves: 2

Ingredients:

- 4 large carrots (300g)
- 1-inch piece fresh ginger (5g)
- 1 tbsp lemon juice (15ml)

Instructions:

1. Juice the carrots and ginger using a juicer.
2. Stir in the lemon juice.
3. Serve immediately.

Nutritional Facts (Per Serving): Calories: 100 | Carbs: 24g | Protein: 2g | Fat: 0g | Fiber: 2g | Sodium: 50mg | Sugars: 18g

Cucumber Mint Smoothie

Prep: 5 minutes | Serves: 2

Ingredients:

- 1 cucumber, chopped (200g)
- 1/2 cup fresh mint leaves (15g)
- 1 apple, cored and chopped (180g)
- 1 cup coconut water (240ml)

Instructions:

1. Place all ingredients in a blender.
2. Blend until smooth.
3. Serve immediately.

Nutritional Facts (Per Serving): Calories: 100 | Carbs: 25g | Protein: 1g | Fat: 0g | Fiber: 4g | Sodium: 50mg | Sugars: 18g

Strawberry Basil Smoothie

Prep: 5 minutes | Serves: 2

Ingredients:

- 1 cup strawberries (150g)
- 1/4 cup fresh basil leaves (10g)
- 1 banana (120g)
- 1 cup almond milk (240ml)

Instructions:

1. Place all ingredients in a blender.
2. Blend until smooth.
3. Serve immediately.

Nutritional Facts (Per Serving): Calories: 200 | Carbs: 45g | Protein: 3g | Fat: 2g | Fiber: 6g | Sodium: 60mg | Sugars: 28g

Watermelon Mint Juice

Prep: 10 minutes | Serves: 2

Ingredients:

- 4 cups watermelon, chopped (600g)
- 1/4 cup fresh mint leaves (10g)

Instructions:

1. Place watermelon and mint leaves in a blender.
2. Blend until smooth.
3. Strain the mixture to remove pulp, if desired.
4. Serve chilled.

Nutritional Facts (Per Serving): Calories: 100 | Carbs: 25g | Protein: 1g | Fat: 0g | Fiber: 1g | Sodium: 5mg | Sugars: 20g

Tropical Sunrise Smoothie

Prep: 5 minutes | Serves: 2

Ingredients:

- 1 cup pineapple, chopped (165g)
- 1 cup mango, chopped (165g)
- 1 cup orange juice (240ml)

Instructions:

1. Place pineapple, mango, and orange juice in a blender.
2. Blend until smooth.
3. Serve immediately.

Nutritional Facts (Per Serving): Calories: 200 | Carbs: 50g | Protein: 2g | Fat: 0g | Fiber: 4g | Sodium: 5mg | Sugars: 40g

CHAPTER 7: LUNCHES:
Hearty Soups and Healthy Stews

Hearty Vegetable and Lentil Stew

Prep: 15 minutes | Cook: 35 minutes | Serves: 4

Ingredients:

- 1 cup dried lentils (200g)
- 4 cups vegetable broth (960ml)
- 2 medium carrots, diced (200g)
- 2 celery stalks, diced (200g)
- 1 medium onion, chopped (150g)
- 2 medium potatoes, diced (400g)
- 1 can diced tomatoes (400g)
- 2 cloves garlic, minced
- 1 tsp dried thyme
- 1 tsp dried rosemary
- 2 tbsp olive oil
- Salt and pepper to taste

Instructions:

1. Heat olive oil in a large pot over medium heat. Add onion and garlic, sauté until soft.
2. Add carrots, celery, and potatoes. Cook for 5 minutes until slightly softened.
3. Stir in lentils, diced tomatoes, vegetable broth, thyme, and rosemary. Bring to a boil.
4. Reduce heat and simmer for 25 minutes until lentils and vegetables are tender.
5. Season with salt and pepper. Serve hot.

Nutritional Facts (Per Serving): Calories: 500 | Sugars: 10g | Fat: 12g | Carbohydrates: 80g | Protein: 20g | Fiber: 20g | Sodium: 600mg

Tuscan White Bean Soup

Prep: 10 minutes | Cook: 30 minutes | Serves: 4

Ingredients:

- 2 cans white beans, drained and rinsed (800g)
- 4 cups vegetable broth (960ml)
- 1 bunch kale, stems removed and chopped (200g)
- 1 can diced tomatoes (400g)
- 1 medium onion, chopped (150g)
- 3 cloves garlic, minced
- 1 tsp dried thyme
- 1 tsp dried rosemary
- 2 tbsp olive oil
- Salt and pepper to taste

Instructions:

1. Heat olive oil in a large pot over medium heat. Add onion and garlic, sauté until fragrant.
2. Add diced tomatoes, white beans, vegetable broth, thyme, and rosemary. Bring to a boil.
3. Reduce heat and add chopped kale. Simmer for 15-20 minutes until kale is tender.
4. Season with salt and pepper. Serve hot.

Nutritional Facts (Per Serving): Calories: 500 | Sugars: 9g | Fat: 14g | Carbohydrates: 75g | Protein: 20g | Fiber: 16g | Sodium: 600mg

Curried Cauliflower and Chickpea Stew

Prep: 10 minutes | Cook: 30 minutes | Serves: 4

Ingredients:

- 1 head cauliflower, chopped (600g)
- 2 cans chickpeas, drained and rinsed (800g)
- 1 can coconut milk (400ml)
- 4 cups vegetable broth (960ml)
- 1 medium onion, chopped (150g)
- 2 cloves garlic, minced
- 2 tbsp curry powder
- 1 tsp ground turmeric
- 2 tbsp olive oil
- Salt and pepper to taste

Instructions:

1. Heat olive oil in a large pot over medium heat. Add onion and garlic, sauté until soft.
2. Add curry powder and turmeric, cook for 1 minute until fragrant.
3. Stir in cauliflower, chickpeas, coconut milk, and vegetable broth. Bring to a boil.
4. Reduce heat and simmer for 20 minutes until cauliflower is tender.
5. Season with salt and pepper. Serve hot.

Nutritional Facts (Per Serving): Calories: 500 | Sugars: 8g | Fat: 20g | Carbohydrates: 60g | Protein: 16g | Fiber: 16g | Sodium: 600mg

Butternut Squash and Chickpea Soup

Prep: 15 minutes | Cook: 45 minutes | Serves: 4

Ingredients:

- 4 cups cubed butternut squash (600g)
- 1 can chickpeas, drained and rinsed (400g)
- 4 cups vegetable broth (960ml)
- 1 medium onion, chopped (150g)
- 2 cloves garlic, minced
- 1 tsp ground cumin
- 1 tsp ground coriander
- 1 tsp smoked paprika
- 2 tbsp olive oil
- Salt and pepper to taste

Instructions:

1. Preheat oven to 400°F (200°C). Toss butternut squash with 1 tbsp olive oil, salt, and pepper. Roast for 25-30 minutes until tender.
2. In a large pot, heat remaining olive oil over medium heat. Add onion and garlic, sauté until translucent.
3. Add roasted butternut squash, chickpeas, vegetable broth, cumin, coriander, and smoked paprika. Bring to a boil, then reduce heat and simmer for 15 minutes.
4. Blend the soup until smooth using an immersion blender or in batches in a regular blender.
5. Adjust seasoning with salt and pepper.

Nutritional Facts (Per Serving): Calories: 500 | Sugars: 10g | Fat: 16g | Carbohydrates: 72g | Protein: 12g | Fiber: 12g | Sodium: 600mg

Creamy Tomato Basil Soup with Orzo

Prep: 10 minutes | Cook: 30 minutes | Serves: 4

Ingredients:

- 4 cups diced tomatoes (960g)
- 1 cup orzo (200g)
- 4 cups vegetable broth (960ml)
- 1 cup coconut milk or cashew cream (240ml)
- 1 medium onion, chopped (150g)
- 2 cloves garlic, minced
- 1 bunch fresh basil, chopped (30g)
- 2 tbsp olive oil
- Salt and pepper to taste

Instructions:

1. Heat olive oil in a large pot over medium heat. Add onion and garlic, sauté until soft.
2. Add diced tomatoes and vegetable broth. Bring to a boil, then reduce heat and simmer for 15 minutes.
3. Stir in orzo and cook for 8-10 minutes until al dente.
4. Add coconut milk or cashew cream and chopped basil. Simmer for another 5 minutes.
5. Season with salt and pepper. Serve hot.

Nutritional Facts (Per Serving): Calories: 500 | Sugars: 10g | Fat: 22g | Carbohydrates: 60g | Protein: 10g | Fiber: 8g | Sodium: 600mg

Spiced Chickpea and Spinach Stew

Prep: 15 minutes | Cook: 30 minutes | Serves: 4

Ingredients:

- 2 cans chickpeas, drained and rinsed (800g)
- 4 cups fresh spinach (120g)
- 1 can diced tomatoes (400g)
- 1 medium onion, chopped (150g)
- 3 cloves garlic, minced
- 2 tsp ground cumin
- 1 tsp ground coriander
- 1 tsp ground turmeric
- 2 tbsp olive oil
- 4 cups vegetable broth (960ml)
- Salt and pepper to taste

Instructions:

1. Heat olive oil in a large pot over medium heat. Add onion and garlic, sauté until soft.
2. Add ground cumin, coriander, and turmeric. Cook for 1 minute until fragrant.
3. Add diced tomatoes, chickpeas, and vegetable broth. Bring to a boil, then reduce heat and simmer for 20 minutes.
4. Stir in fresh spinach and cook until wilted, about 2 minutes.
5. Season with salt and pepper. Serve hot.

Nutritional Facts (Per Serving): Calories: 500 | Sugars: 10g | Fat: 14g | Carbohydrates: 76g | Protein: 18g | Fiber: 16g | Sodium: 600mg

Hearty Vegetable and Quinoa Soup

Prep: 15 minutes | Cook: 30 minutes | Serves: 4

Ingredients:

- 1 cup quinoa (185g)
- 4 cups vegetable broth (960ml)
- 2 medium carrots, diced (200g)
- 2 celery stalks, diced (200g)
- 1 medium onion, chopped (150g)
- 1 zucchini, diced (200g)
- 1 can diced tomatoes (400g)
- 2 cloves garlic, minced
- 1 tsp dried thyme
- 1 tsp dried oregano
- 2 tbsp olive oil
- Salt and pepper to taste

Instructions:

1. Rinse quinoa under cold water. Set aside.
2. Heat olive oil in a large pot over medium heat. Add onion and garlic, sauté until soft.
3. Add carrots, celery, and zucchini. Cook for 5 minutes until slightly softened.
4. Stir in quinoa, diced tomatoes, vegetable broth, thyme, and oregano. Bring to a boil.
5. Reduce heat and simmer for 20 minutes until quinoa and vegetables are tender.
6. Season with salt and pepper. Serve hot.

Nutritional Facts (Per Serving): Calories: 500 | Sugars: 9g | Fat: 14g | Carbohydrates: 80g | Protein: 15g | Fiber: 12g | Sodium: 600mg

Zucchini and White Bean Stew

Prep: 10 minutes | Cook: 25 minutes | Serves: 4

Ingredients:

- 2 cans white beans, drained and rinsed (800g)
- 2 medium zucchinis, diced (400g)
- 1 can diced tomatoes (400g)
- 1 medium onion, chopped (150g)
- 3 cloves garlic, minced
- 1 tsp dried basil
- 1 tsp dried oregano
- 2 tbsp olive oil
- 4 cups vegetable broth (960ml)
- Salt and pepper to taste

Instructions:

1. Heat olive oil in a large pot over medium heat. Add onion and garlic, sauté until soft.
2. Add diced zucchinis and cook for 5 minutes until slightly softened.
3. Stir in white beans, diced tomatoes, vegetable broth, basil, and oregano. Bring to a boil.
4. Reduce heat and simmer for 15 minutes until vegetables are tender.
5. Season with salt and pepper. Serve hot.

Nutritional Facts (Per Serving): Calories: 500 | Sugars: 8g | Fat: 14g | Carbohydrates: 70g | Protein: 20g | Fiber: 15g | Sodium: 600mg

Smoky Eggplant and Tomato Stew

Prep: 15 minutes | Cook: 30 minutes | Serves: 4

Ingredients:

- 2 medium eggplants, diced (600g)
- 1 can diced tomatoes (400g)
- 1 medium onion, chopped (150g)
- 2 cloves garlic, minced
- 1 red bell pepper, diced (150g)
- 4 cups vegetable broth (960ml)
- 1 tsp smoked paprika
- 1 tsp ground cumin
- 2 tbsp olive oil
- Salt and pepper to taste

Instructions:

1. Heat olive oil in a large pot over medium heat. Add onion and garlic, sauté until soft.
2. Add diced eggplant and red bell pepper, cook for 5 minutes until slightly softened.
3. Stir in diced tomatoes, vegetable broth, smoked paprika, and cumin. Bring to a boil.
4. Reduce heat and simmer for 20 minutes until vegetables are tender.
5. Season with salt and pepper. Serve hot.

Nutritional Facts (Per Serving): Calories: 500 | Sugars: 10g | Fat: 14g | Carbohydrates: 75g | Protein: 10g | Fiber: 18g | Sodium: 600mg

Butternut Squash and Quinoa Stew

Prep: 15 minutes | Cook: 30 minutes | Serves: 4

Ingredients:

- 4 cups butternut squash, diced (600g)
- 1 cup quinoa (185g)
- 4 cups vegetable broth (960ml)
- 1 medium onion, chopped (150g)
- 2 cloves garlic, minced
- 1 can diced tomatoes (400g)
- 2 tsp ground cumin
- 1 tsp ground coriander
- 2 tbsp olive oil
- Salt and pepper to taste

Instructions:

1. Heat olive oil in a large pot over medium heat. Add onion and garlic, sauté until soft.
2. Add diced butternut squash, cook for 5 minutes until slightly softened.
3. Stir in quinoa, diced tomatoes, vegetable broth, cumin, and coriander. Bring to a boil.
4. Reduce heat and simmer for 20 minutes until quinoa and squash are tender.
5. Season with salt and pepper. Serve hot.

Nutritional Facts (Per Serving): Calories: 500 | Sugars: 10g | Fat: 14g | Carbohydrates: 80g | Protein: 12g | Fiber: 12g | Sodium: 600mg

CHAPTER 8: LUNCHES: Nutritious Grain and Legume Dishes

Quinoa and Black Bean Salad with Avocado

Prep: 15 minutes | Cook: 15 minutes | Serves: 4

Ingredients:

- 1 cup quinoa (185g)
- 1 can black beans, drained and rinsed (400g)
- 1 avocado, diced (200g)
- 1 cup cherry tomatoes, halved (200g)
- 1 small red onion, diced (100g)
- 1 red bell pepper, diced (150g)
- 1/4 cup fresh cilantro, chopped (10g)
- Juice of 2 limes
- 2 tbsp olive oil
- Salt and pepper to taste

Instructions:

1. Cook quinoa and let it cool.
2. Mix cooled quinoa, black beans, avocado, cherry tomatoes, red onion, red bell pepper, and cilantro in a large bowl.
3. Whisk lime juice, olive oil, salt, and pepper in a small bowl. Pour over the salad and toss.
4. Serve chilled or at room temperature.

Nutritional Facts (Per Serving): Calories: 500 | Sugars: 5g | Fat: 20g | Carbohydrates: 65g | Protein: 12g | Fiber: 15g | Sodium: 400mg

Red Lentil and Quinoa Patties

Prep: 15 minutes | Cook: 20 minutes | Serves: 4

Ingredients:

- 1 cup red lentils (200g)
- 1/2 cup quinoa (90g)
- 1 medium carrot, grated (100g)
- 1 small onion, finely chopped (100g)
- 2 cloves garlic, minced
- 1 tsp ground cumin
- 1 tsp smoked paprika
- 1/4 cup gluten-free breadcrumbs or ground gluten-free oats.
- 2 tbsp olive oil
- Salt and pepper to taste

Instructions:

1. Cook red lentils and quinoa, then let cool.
2. Mix lentils, quinoa, grated carrot, onion, garlic, cumin, smoked paprika, breadcrumbs, salt, and pepper in a bowl.
3. Form patties from the mixture.
4. Cook patties in a skillet with olive oil for 4-5 minutes per side until golden brown.
5. Serve hot with a side salad or yogurt sauce if desired.

Nutritional Facts (Per Serving): Calories: 500 | Sugars: 4g | Fat: 14g | Carbohydrates: 75g | Protein: 18g | Fiber: 16g | Sodium: 600mg

Chickpea and Spinach Pilaf

Prep: 10 minutes | Cook: 30 minutes | Serves: 4

Ingredients:

- 1 cup basmati rice (185g)
- 1 can chickpeas, drained and rinsed (400g)
- 4 cups fresh spinach (120g)
- 1 medium onion, chopped (150g)
- 2 cloves garlic, minced
- 1 tsp ground cumin
- 1 tsp ground coriander
- 2 cups vegetable broth (480ml)
- 2 tbsp olive oil
- Salt and pepper to taste

Instructions:

1. Heat olive oil in a large pot over medium heat. Add onion and garlic, sauté until soft.
2. Add ground cumin and coriander, cook for 1 minute until fragrant.
3. Stir in rice, chickpeas, and vegetable broth. Bring to a boil.
4. Reduce heat, cover, and simmer for 15-20 minutes until rice is cooked.
5. Add spinach and cook until wilted, about 2 minutes.
6. Season with salt and pepper. Serve hot.

Nutritional Facts (Per Serving): Calories: 500 | Sugars: 5g | Fat: 14g | Carbohydrates: 75g | Protein: 12g | Fiber: 10g | Sodium: 600mg

Millet and Vegetable Bowl

Prep: 15 minutes | Cook: 25 minutes | Serves: 4

Ingredients:

- 1 cup millet (170g)
- 1 medium zucchini, diced (200g)
- 1 red bell pepper, diced (150g)
- 1 cup cherry tomatoes, halved (200g)
- 1 medium carrot, diced (100g)
- 1 medium onion, chopped (150g)
- 2 cups vegetable broth (480ml)
- 2 tbsp olive oil
- 1 tsp ground cumin
- 1 tsp ground paprika
- Salt and pepper to taste

Instructions:

1. Heat olive oil in a large pot over medium heat. Add onion and garlic, sauté until soft.
2. Add zucchini, bell pepper, carrot, and cherry tomatoes. Cook for 5 minutes until slightly softened.
3. Stir in millet, vegetable broth, cumin, and paprika. Bring to a boil.
4. Remove from heat, cover, and let sit for 10 minutes until millet absorbs the liquid.
5. Fluff millet with a fork. Season with salt and pepper. Serve warm.

Nutritional Facts (Per Serving): Calories: 500 | Sugars: 8g | Fat: 12g | Carbohydrates: 80g | Protein: 14g | Fiber: 12g | Sodium: 600mg

CHAPTER 9: LUNCHES:
Comforting Pasta and Rice Dishes

Creamy Spinach and Mushroom Pasta

Prep: 15 minutes | Cook: 20 minutes | Serves: 4

Ingredients:

- 8 oz gluten-free whole grain pasta (225g)
- 1 cup raw cashews, soaked (150g)
- 1 cup water (240ml)
- 4 cups fresh spinach (120g)
- 1 cup mushrooms, sliced (150g)
- 1 medium onion, chopped (150g)
- 2 cloves garlic, minced
- 2 tbsp olive oil
- 1 tbsp nutritional yeast
- Salt and pepper to taste

Instructions:

1. Cook pasta and set aside. Blend soaked cashews with water to make cream.

3. Sauté onion and garlic in olive oil, add mushrooms, and cook for 5 minutes.

4. Stir in cashew cream and nutritional yeast, cook for 2 minutes.

5. Add spinach and pasta, toss until spinach wilts and pasta is coated.

Nutritional Facts (Per Serving): Calories: 500 | Sugars: 5g | Fat: 18g | Carbohydrates: 70g | Protein: 15g | Fiber: 10g | Sodium: 400mg

Avocado Basil Pesto Pasta

Prep: 10 minutes | Cook: 10 minutes | Serves: 4

Ingredients:

- 8 oz gluten-free whole grain pasta (225g)
- 1 cup fresh basil leaves (30g)
- 1/4 cup nutritional yeast or vegan Parmesan cheese (30g)
- 2 cloves garlic
- Juice of 1 lemon
- 1/4 cup olive oil (60ml)
- Salt and pepper to taste
- 2 ripe avocados (300g)

Instructions:

1. Cook pasta according to package instructions. Drain and set aside.

2. In a food processor, blend avocados, basil, nutritional yeast or vegan Parmesan, garlic, lemon juice, and olive oil until smooth.

3. Toss the cooked pasta with the avocado basil pesto. Season with salt and pepper.

4. Serve immediately, garnished with extra basil leaves if desired.

Nutritional Facts (Per Serving): Calories: 500 | Sugars: 2g | Fat: 25g | Carbohydrates: 60g | Protein: 10g | Fiber: 10g | Sodium: 200mg

Spaghetti with Lentil Bolognese

Prep: 10 minutes | Cook: 40 minutes | Serves: 4

Ingredients:

- 8 oz gluten-free spaghetti (225g)
- 1 cup dried lentils (200g)
- 1 can diced tomatoes (400g)
- 1 medium onion, chopped (150g)
- 2 cloves garlic, minced
- 2 tbsp tomato paste
- 1 carrot, diced (100g)
- 1 celery stalk, diced (100g)
- 2 cups vegetable broth (480ml)
- 2 tbsp olive oil
- 1 tsp dried oregano
- 1 tsp dried basil
- Salt and pepper to taste

Instructions:

1. Cook lentils according to package instructions. Set aside.
2. Heat olive oil in a large pot over medium heat. Add onion, garlic, carrot, and celery, sauté until soft.
3. Stir in tomato paste, diced tomatoes, cooked lentils, vegetable broth, oregano, and basil. Simmer for 20 minutes until thickened.
4. Cook spaghetti according to package instructions. Drain and set aside.
5. Serve lentil bolognese sauce over spaghetti. Season with salt and pepper.

Nutritional Facts (Per Serving): Calories: 500 | Sugars: 7g | Fat: 12g | Carbohydrates: 80g | Protein: 20g | Fiber: 15g | Sodium: 600mg

Lemon Asparagus Risotto

Prep: 10 minutes | Cook: 30 minutes | Serves: 4

Ingredients:

- 1 cup Arborio rice (200g)
- 1 bunch asparagus, trimmed and cut into 1-inch pieces (300g)
- 1 medium onion, chopped (150g)
- 2 cloves garlic, minced
- 4 cups vegetable broth (960ml)
- 1/2 cup dry white wine (120ml)
- 1/4 cup nutritional yeast or vegan Parmesan cheese (30g)
- Juice and zest of 1 lemon
- 2 tbsp olive oil
- Salt and pepper to taste

Instructions:

1. Sauté onion and garlic in olive oil.
2. Add Arborio rice and cook for 2 minutes.
3. Pour in white wine and let it absorb. Gradually add vegetable broth, stirring until absorbed.
4. Stir in asparagus and cook until tender.
5. Add nutritional yeast or vegan Parmesan, lemon juice, zest, salt, and pepper. Mix well.

Nutritional Facts (Per Serving): Calories: 500 | Sugars: 4g | Fat: 14g | Carbohydrates: 75g | Protein: 12g | Fiber: 5g | Sodium: 600mg

Butternut Squash and Sage Risotto

Prep: 15 minutes | Cook: 30 minutes | Serves: 4

Ingredients:

- 1 cup Arborio rice (200g)
- 2 cups butternut squash, diced (300g)
- 1 medium onion, chopped (150g)
- 2 cloves garlic, minced
- 4 cups vegetable broth (960ml)
- 1/2 cup dry white wine (120ml)
- 1/4 cup nutritional yeast or vegan Parmesan cheese (30g)
- 1 tbsp fresh sage, chopped
- 2 tbsp olive oil
- Salt and pepper to taste

Instructions:

1. Heat olive oil in a large pot over medium heat. Add onion and garlic, sauté until soft.
2. Add Arborio rice and cook for 2 minutes until lightly toasted.
3. Pour in white wine and cook until absorbed.
4. Gradually add vegetable broth, one cup at a time, stirring constantly until each addition is absorbed before adding the next.
5. When the rice is halfway cooked, stir in butternut squash and cook until tender.
6. Add nutritional yeast or vegan Parmesan, fresh sage, salt, and pepper. Mix well.

Nutritional Facts (Per Serving): Calories: 500 | Sugars: 6g | Fat: 14g | Carbohydrates: 80g | Protein: 12g | Fiber: 4g | Sodium: 600mg

Spinach and Artichoke Risotto

Prep: 15 minutes | Cook: 30 minutes | Serves: 4

Ingredients:

- 1 cup Arborio rice (200g)
- 1 cup fresh spinach, chopped (30g)
- 1 can artichoke hearts, drained and chopped (400g)
- 1 medium onion, chopped (150g)
- 2 cloves garlic, mince
- 4 cups vegetable broth (960ml)
- 1/2 cup dry white wine (120ml)
- 1/4 cup nutritional yeast or vegan Parmesan cheese (30g)
- 2 tbsp olive oil
- Salt and pepper to taste

Instructions:

1. Heat olive oil in a large pot over medium heat. Add onion and garlic, sauté until soft.
2. Add Arborio rice and cook for 2 minutes until lightly toasted.
3. Pour in white wine and cook until absorbed.
4. Gradually add vegetable broth, one cup at a time, stirring constantly until each addition is absorbed before adding the next.
5. When the rice is almost cooked, stir in spinach and artichoke hearts. Cook until heated through.
6. Add nutritional yeast or vegan Parmesan, salt, and pepper. Mix well.

Nutritional Facts (Per Serving): Calories: 500 | Sugars: 3g | Fat: 14g | Carbohydrates: 80g | Protein: 12g | Fiber: 8g | Sodium: 600mg

CHAPTER 10: LUNCHES: Healthy Casseroles and Pies

Sweet Potato Shepherd's Pie

Prep: 20 minutes | Cook: 40 minutes | Serves: 4

Ingredients:

- 2 large sweet potatoes, peeled and cubed (600g)
- 1 cup lentils (200g)
- 1 medium onion, chopped (150g)
- 2 cloves garlic, minced
- 2 medium carrots, diced (200g)
- 1 cup frozen peas (150g)
- 1 cup vegetable broth (240ml)
- 1 tbsp tomato paste
- 1 tbsp soy sauce
- 2 tbsp olive oil
- Salt and pepper to taste

Instructions:

1. Preheat oven to 400°F (200°C).
2. Boil and mash sweet potatoes with salt, pepper, and olive oil.
3. Cook lentils as directed.
4. Sauté onion, garlic, and carrots in olive oil, then add lentils, tomato paste, soy sauce, and broth. Cook until thickened, then add peas.
5. Spread lentil mixture in a baking dish, top with mashed sweet potatoes.
6. Bake for 20 minutes until golden. Serve hot.

Nutritional Facts (Per Serving): Calories: 500 | Sugars: 10g | Fat: 12g | Carbohydrates: 85g | Protein: 14g | Fiber: 16g | Sodium: 600mg

Broccoli and Rice Casserole

Prep: 15 minutes | Cook: 40 minutes | Serves: 4

Ingredients:

- 1 cup brown rice (185g)
- 2 cups broccoli florets (300g)
- 1 cup raw cashews, soaked (150g)
- 1 cup water (240ml)
- 1/4 cup nutritional yeast (20g)
- 1 medium onion, chopped (150g)
- 2 cloves garlic, minced
- 2 tbsp olive oil
- Salt and pepper to taste

Instructions:

1. Cook brown rice and preheat oven to 375°F (190°C).
Steam broccoli until tender.
Blend soaked cashews, water, nutritional yeast, salt, and pepper to make cashew cheese sauce.
Sauté onion and garlic in olive oil.
Mix rice, broccoli, sautéed onion, garlic, and cashew sauce in a bowl. Transfer to a baking dish.
Bake for 20-25 minutes until golden. Serve hot.

Nutritional Facts (Per Serving): Calories: 500 | Sugars: 4g | Fat: 18g | Carbohydrates: 70g | Protein: 14g | Fiber: 8g | Sodium: 400mg

Eggplant and Lentil Moussaka

Prep: 20 minutes | Cook: 60 minutes | Serves: 4

Ingredients:

- 2 large eggplants, sliced (600g)
- 1 cup lentils (200g)
- 1 can diced tomatoes (400g)
- 1 medium onion, chopped (150g)
- 2 cloves garlic, minced
- 1 cup water (240ml)
- 1/2 cup raw cashews, soaked (75g)
- 1/4 cup nutritional yeast (20g)
- 2 tbsp olive oil
- 1 tsp dried oregano
- 1 tsp dried basil
- Salt and pepper to taste

Instructions:

1. Preheat oven to 375°F (190°C). Brush eggplant slices with olive oil and bake for 20 minutes until soft.
2. Cook lentils as directed.
3. Sauté onion and garlic in olive oil, then add diced tomatoes, lentils, oregano, basil, salt, and pepper. Simmer for 15 minutes.
4. Blend soaked cashews with water, nutritional yeast, salt, and pepper for a creamy topping.
5. Layer eggplant, lentil mixture, and creamy topping in a baking dish.
6. Bake for 30 minutes until golden.

Nutritional Facts (Per Serving): Calories: 500 | Sugars: 9g | Fat: 16g | Carbohydrates: 70g | Protein: 18g | Fiber: 14g | Sodium: 600mg

Spinach and Mushroom Lasagna

Prep: 20 minutes | Cook: 40 minutes | Serves: 4

Ingredients:

- 8 oz gluten-free lasagna noodles (225g)
- 2 cups fresh spinach, chopped (60g)
- 2 cups mushrooms, sliced (300g)
- 1 medium onion, chopped (150g)
- 2 cloves garlic, minced
- 1 cup raw cashews, soaked (150g)
- 1 cup water (240ml)
- 1/4 cup nutritional yeast (20g)
- 2 cups marinara sauce (480ml)
- 2 tbsp olive oil
- Salt and pepper to taste

Instructions:

1. Preheat oven to 375°F (190°C). Cook lasagna gluten-free noodles.
2. Sauté onion, garlic, and mushrooms in olive oil, add spinach, and cook until wilted. Season with salt and pepper.
3. Blend soaked cashews, water, nutritional yeast, salt, and pepper for the cashew cream sauce.
4. Layer marinara sauce, noodles, mushroom-spinach mix, and cashew cream in a baking dish. Repeat, finishing with marinara.
5. Bake for 30 minutes until bubbly and golden.

Nutritional Facts (Per Serving): Calories: 500 | Sugars: 10g | Fat: 18g | Carbohydrates: 70g | Protein: 14g | Fiber: 8g | Sodium: 600mg

CHAPTER 11: LUNCHES:
Vegetable Pitas, Burgers, Quesadillas

Black Bean Burger with Avocado

Prep: 15 minutes | Cook: 15 minutes | Serves: 4

Ingredients:

- 1 can black beans, drained and rinsed (400g)
- 1/2 cup gluten-free breadcrumbs (60g)
- 1/4 cup chopped onion (40g)
- 1 clove garlic, mince
- 1 tsp ground cumin
- 2 tbsp ground flaxseed mixed with 6 tbsp water
- 1 tbsp olive oil
- 4 gluten-free whole grain buns (300g)
- 1 avocado, sliced (200g)
- Salt and pepper to taste
- 1 tsp smoked paprika

Instructions:

1. In a bowl, mash black beans with a fork until mostly smooth. Stir in flax egg, breadcrumbs, onion, garlic, cumin, paprika, salt, and pepper until well combined. Form mixture into 4 patties.
3. Heat olive oil in a skillet over medium heat. Cook patties for 4-5 minutes per side until browned and heated through.
4. Serve each patty on a whole grain bun topped with avocado slices.

Nutritional Facts (Per Serving): Calories: 500 | Sugars: 4g | Fat: 18g | Carbohydrates: 65g | Protein: 14g | Fiber: 12g | Sodium: 500mg

Hummus and Veggie Pita

Prep: 10 minutes | Cook: 15 minutes | Serves: 4

Ingredients:

- 4 gluten-free whole grain pitas (240g)
- 1 cup hummus (240g)
- 1 cucumber, sliced (200g)
- 1 red bell pepper, sliced (150g)
- 1 cup shredded carrots (100g)
- 1/4 cup chopped fresh parsley (15g)
- Salt and pepper to taste

Instructions:

1. Slice pitas in half to form pockets.
2. Spread hummus inside each pita half.
3. Fill with cucumber, red bell pepper, shredded carrots, and parsley.
4. Season with salt and pepper. Serve immediately.

Nutritional Facts (Per Serving): Calories: 500 | Sugars: 5g | Fat: 16g | Carbohydrates: 75g | Protein: 14g | Fiber: 12g | Sodium: 600mg

Portobello Mushroom Burger

Prep: 10 minutes | Cook: 15 minutes | Serves: 4

Ingredients:

- 4 large portobello mushrooms (600g)
- 4 gluten-free whole grain buns (300g) or lettuce wraps.
- 4 lettuce leaves (60g)
- 2 tbsp olive oil
- 1 large tomato, sliced (200g)
- 1 tbsp balsamic vinegar
- Salt and pepper to taste

Instructions:

1. Preheat grill to medium heat.
2. Remove stems from portobello mushrooms and brush with olive oil and balsamic vinegar. Season with salt and pepper.
3. Grill mushrooms for 5-7 minutes per side until tender.
4. Serve each mushroom on a whole grain bun with lettuce and tomato slices.

Nutritional Facts (Per Serving): Calories: 500 | Sugars: 7g | Fat: 18g | Carbohydrates: 70g | Protein: 12g | Fiber: 8g | Sodium: 600mg

Zucchini and Corn Pita

Prep: 10 minutes | Cook: 15 minutes | Serves: 4

Ingredients:

- 2 medium zucchinis, sliced (400g)
- 1 cup corn kernels (160g)
- 4 gluten-free whole wheat pitas (240g)
- 1 cup salsa (240g)
- 2 tbsp olive oil
- Salt and pepper to taste

Instructions:

1. Preheat grill to medium heat.
2. Toss zucchini slices and corn kernels with olive oil, salt, and pepper.
3. Grill zucchini and corn until tender, about 5-7 minutes.
4. Warm pitas on the grill for 1-2 minutes per side.
5. Fill each pita with grilled zucchini and corn, topping with salsa.

Nutritional Facts (Per Serving): Calories: 500 | Sugars: 6g | Fat: 14g | Carbohydrates: 80g | Protein: 14g | Fiber: 10g | Sodium: 600mg

CHAPTER 12: SNACK:
Healthy, Quick and Tasty Snacks

Jalapeño Lime Hummus with Rice Crackers

Prep: 10 minutes | Cook: 10 minutes | Serves: 4

Ingredients:

- 1 cup canned chickpeas, drained and rinsed (240g)
- 1/4 cup tahini (60g)
- 2 tbsp olive oil (30ml)
- 1 tbsp fresh lime juice (15ml)
- 1 clove garlic, minced
- 1 fresh jalapeño, seeded and chopped
- 1/2 tsp ground cumin (2g)
- Salt to taste
- 1 pack gluten-free rice crackers (100g)

Instructions:

1. In a food processor, combine chickpeas, tahini, olive oil, lime juice, garlic, jalapeño, and cumin. Blend until smooth.
2. Season with salt to taste and blend again until fully mixed.
3. Serve with rice crackers.

Nutritional Facts (Per Serving): Calories: 220 | Sugars: 1g | Fat: 14g | Carbohydrates: 18g | Protein: 6g | Fiber: 4g | Sodium: 200mg

Avocado and Cilantro Hummus with Veggie Sticks

Prep: 10 minutes | Cook: 10 minutes | Serves: 4

Ingredients:

- 1 cup canned chickpeas, drained and rinsed (240g)
- 1 ripe avocado, peeled and pitted (200g)
- 1/4 cup fresh cilantro, chopped (15g)
- 2 tbsp olive oil (30ml)
- 1 tbsp lime juice (15ml)
- 1 clove garlic, minced
- Salt to taste
- Assorted veggie sticks (carrots, cucumbers, bell peppers) (300g)

Instructions:

1. In a food processor, combine chickpeas, avocado, cilantro, olive oil, lime juice, and garlic. Blend until smooth.
2. Season with salt to taste and blend again until fully mixed.
3. Serve with assorted veggie sticks.

Nutritional Facts (Per Serving): Calories: 220 | Sugars: 2g | Fat: 16g | Carbohydrates: 17g | Protein: 4g | Fiber: 6g | Sodium: 150mg

Beetroot Hummus with Multigrain Flatbread

Prep: 10 minutes | Cook: 10 minutes | Serves: 4

Ingredients:

- 1 cup canned chickpeas, drained and rinsed (240g)
- 1 small cooked beetroot, chopped (150g)
- 1/4 cup tahini (60g)
- 2 tbsp olive oil (30ml)
- 1 tbsp lemon juice (15ml)
- 1 clove garlic, minced
- Salt to taste
- 4 pieces multigrain flatbread (200g)

Instructions:

1. In a food processor, combine chickpeas, beetroot, tahini, olive oil, lemon juice, and garlic. Blend until smooth.
2. Season with salt to taste and blend again until fully mixed.
3. Serve with multigrain gluten-free flatbread or gluten-free crackers.

Nutritional Facts (Per Serving): Calories: 220 | Sugars: 3g | Fat: 12g | Carbohydrates: 25g | Protein: 5g | Fiber: 5g | Sodium: 180mg

Cumin-Spiced Falafel

Prep: 15 minutes | Cook: 25 minutes | Serves: 4

Ingredients:

- 1 cup canned chickpeas, drained and rinsed (240g)
- 1/4 cup chopped onion (40g)
- 2 tbsp fresh parsley, chopped (8g)
- 1 clove garlic, minced
- 1 tsp ground cumin (4g)
- 1 tsp ground coriander (4g)
- 1/2 tsp gluten-free baking powder (2g)
- 1 tbsp olive oil (15ml)
- Salt to taste

Instructions:

1. Preheat oven to 375°F (190°C).
2. In a food processor, combine chickpeas, onion, parsley, garlic, cumin, coriander, and baking powder. Blend until smooth.
3. Form mixture into small balls and place on a baking sheet lined with parchment paper.
4. Brush falafel balls with olive oil and bake for 20-25 minutes, until golden brown.
5. Serve warm.

Nutritional Facts (Per Serving): Calories: 220 | Sugars: 2g | Fat: 8g | Carbohydrates: 30g | Protein: 7g | Fiber: 6g | Sodium: 300mg

Sun-Dried Tomato and Basil Hummus with Pita Chips

Prep: 10 minutes | Cook: 15 minutes | Serves: 4

Ingredients:

- 1 cup canned chickpeas, drained and rinsed (240g)
- 1/4 cup sun-dried tomatoes in oil, drained (40g)
- 1/4 cup fresh basil leaves (15g)
- 2 tbsp tahini (30g)
- 2 tbsp olive oil (30ml)
- 1 clove garlic, minced
- 1 tbsp lemon juice (15ml)
- Salt to taste
- 4 gluten-free pita chips (200g)

Instructions:

1. In a food processor, combine chickpeas, sun-dried tomatoes, basil, tahini, olive oil, garlic, and lemon juice. Blend until smooth.
2. Season with salt to taste and blend again until fully mixed.
3. Serve with gluten-free pita chips.

Nutritional Facts (Per Serving): Calories: 220 | Sugars: 3g | Fat: 10g | Carbohydrates: 26g | Protein: 5g | Fiber: 5g | Sodium: 250mg

Pumpkin and Sage Hummus with Cucumber Slices

Prep: 10 minutes | Cook: 15 minutes || Serves: 4

Ingredients:

- 1 cup canned chickpeas, drained and rinsed (240g)
- 1/2 cup pumpkin puree (120g)
- 1 tbsp fresh sage, chopped (5g)
- 2 tbsp tahini (30g)
- 2 tbsp olive oil (30ml)
- 1 clove garlic, minced
- 1 tbsp lemon juice (15ml)
- Salt to taste
- 1 large cucumber, sliced (300g)

Instructions:

1. In a food processor, combine chickpeas, pumpkin puree, sage, tahini, olive oil, garlic, and lemon juice. Blend until smooth.
2. Season with salt to taste and blend again until fully mixed.
3. Serve with cucumber slices.

Nutritional Facts (Per Serving): Calories: 220 | Sugars: 2g | Fat: 12g | Carbohydrates: 22g | Protein: 5g | Fiber: 6g | Sodium: 200mg

Smoky Eggplant Baba Ganoush with Whole Wheat Pita

Prep: 10 minutes | Cook: 30 minutes | Serves: 4

Ingredients:

- 1 large eggplant (500g)
- 1/4 cup tahini (60g)
- 2 tbsp lemon juice (30ml)
- 2 tbsp olive oil (30ml)
- 2 cloves garlic, minced
- 1/2 tsp smoked paprika (2g)
- Salt to taste
- 4 gluten-free pita breads (240g)

Instructions:

1. Preheat oven to 400°F (200°C). Roast the eggplant until the skin is charred and the flesh is soft, about 30 minutes. Let cool.
2. Scoop out the eggplant flesh and place in a food processor. Add tahini, lemon juice, olive oil, garlic, smoked paprika, and salt. Blend until smooth.
3. Serve with gluten-free pita bread.

Nutritional Facts (Per Serving): Calories: 220 | Sugars: 3g | Fat: 11g | Carbohydrates: 26g | Protein: 5g | Fiber: 7g | Sodium: 200mg

Mini Bell Peppers Stuffed with Guacamole

Prep: 10 minutes | Cook: 15 minutes | Serves: 4

Ingredients:

- 8 mini bell peppers (200g)
- 2 ripe avocados, peeled and pitted (400g)
- 1 small tomato, finely chopped (100g)
- 1/4 cup red onion, finely chopped (40g)
- 2 tbsp fresh lime juice (30ml)
- 1 tbsp chopped cilantro (5g)
- Salt to taste

Instructions:

1. In a bowl, mash avocados and mix in tomato, red onion, lime juice, cilantro, and salt to make guacamole.
2. Cut mini bell peppers in half and remove seeds.
3. Stuff each bell pepper half with guacamole.

Nutritional Facts (Per Serving): Calories: 220 | Sugars: 2g | Fat: 18g | Carbohydrates: 16g | Protein: 3g | Fiber: 8g | Sodium: 150mg

CHAPTER 13: SNACK:
Energy bars: prepare in advance

Fig and Hazelnut Bars

Prep:10 minutes | Cook: 25 minutes | Serves: 4

Ingredients:

- 1 cup dried figs (150g)
- 1/2 cup hazelnuts (70g)
- 1/2 cup rolled oats (45g)
- 2 tbsp low carb sweeteners (30g)

Instructions:

1. In a food processor, blend dried figs, hazelnuts, rolled oats, and low carb sweeteners until the mixture is sticky and well combined.
2. Press the mixture into a parchment-lined baking dish and refrigerate for at least 1 hour.
3. Cut into bars and serve.

Nutritional Facts (Per Serving): Calories: 220 | Sugars: 16g | Fat: 10g | Carbohydrates: 30g | Protein: 4g | Fiber: 5g | Sodium: 5mg

Blueberry Almond Bars

Prep: 10 minutes | Cook: 25 minutes | Serves: 4

Ingredients:

- 1 cup dried blueberries (150g)
- 1/2 cup almonds (70g)
- 1/2 cup rolled oats (45g)
- 2 tbsp low carb sweeteners (30g)

Instructions:

1. In a food processor, blend dried blueberries, almonds, rolled oats, and low carb sweeteners until the mixture is sticky and well combined.
2. Press the mixture into a parchment-lined baking dish and refrigerate for at least 1 hour.
3. Cut into bars and serve.

Nutritional Facts (Per Serving): Calories: 220 | Sugars: 16g | Fat: 10g | Carbohydrates: 30g | Protein: 4g | Fiber: 5g | Sodium: 5mg

Cherry Cashew Bars

Prep: 10 minutes | Cook: 25 minutes | Serves: 4

Ingredients:

- 1 cup dried cherries (150g)
- 1/2 cup cashews (70g)
- 1/2 cup rolled oats (45g)
- 2 tbsp low carb sweeteners (30g)

Instructions:

1. In a food processor, blend dried cherries, cashews, rolled oats, and low carb sweeteners until the mixture is sticky and well combined.
2. Press the mixture into a parchment-lined baking dish and refrigerate for at least 1 hour.
3. Cut into bars and serve.

Nutritional Facts (Per Serving): Calories: 220 | Sugars: 16g | Fat: 10g | Carbohydrates: 30g | Protein: 4g | Fiber: 5g | Sodium: 5mg

Cranberry Pistachio Bars

Prep: 10 minutes | Cook: 25 minutes | Serves: 4

Ingredients:

- 1 cup dried cranberries (150g)
- 1/2 cup pistachios (70g)
- 1/2 cup rolled oats (45g)
- 2 tbsp low carb sweeteners (30g)

Instructions:

1. In a food processor, blend dried cranberries, pistachios, rolled oats, and low carb sweeteners until the mixture is sticky and well combined.
2. Press the mixture into a parchment-lined baking dish and refrigerate for at least 1 hour.
3. Cut into bars and serve.

Nutritional Facts (Per Serving): Calories: 220 | Sugars: 16g | Fat: 10g | Carbohydrates: 30g | Protein: 4g | Fiber: 5g | Sodium: 5mg

CHAPTER 14: DESSERT:
Healthy Vegan Desserts

Avocado Chocolate Mousse

Prep: 10 minutes | Cook: 15 minutes | Serves: 4

Ingredients:

- 2 ripe avocados (400g)
- 1/4 cup unsweetened cocoa powder (30g)
- 1/4 cup low carb sweeteners (30g)
- 1/4 cup almond milk (60ml)
- 1 tsp vanilla extract (5ml)

Instructions:

1. In a blender, combine avocados, cocoa powder, low carb sweeteners, almond milk, and vanilla extract. Blend until smooth.
2. Chill in the refrigerator for at least 30 minutes before serving.

Nutritional Facts (Per Serving): Calories: 220 | Sugars: 1g | Fat: 15g | Carbohydrates: 20g | Protein: 3g | Fiber: 9g | Sodium: 10mg

Chia Seed Pudding with Mixed Berries

Prep: 10 minutes | Cook: 10 minutes | Serves: 4

Ingredients:

- 1/4 cup chia seeds (40g)
- 1 cup almond milk (240ml)
- 2 tbsp low carb sweeteners (30g)
- 1/2 tsp vanilla extract (2.5ml)
- 1 cup mixed berries (150g)

Instructions:

1. In a bowl, mix chia seeds, almond milk, low carb sweeteners, and vanilla extract. Stir well to combine.
2. Refrigerate for at least 4 hours or overnight until thickened.
3. Serve topped with mixed berries.

Nutritional Facts (Per Serving): Calories: 220 | Sugars: 7g | Fat: 10g | Carbohydrates: 30g | Protein: 5g | Fiber: 11g | Sodium: 60mg

Coconut Milk Panna Cotta with Mango

Prep: 10 minutes | Cook: 5 minutes | Serves: 4

Ingredients:

- 1 can coconut milk (400ml)
- 1/4 cup low carb sweeteners (30g)
- 1 tsp agar-agar powder (5g)
- 1 tsp vanilla extract (5ml)
- 1 ripe mango, diced (200g)

Instructions:

1. In a saucepan, combine coconut milk, low carb sweeteners, and agar-agar powder. Bring to a boil over medium heat, stirring constantly.
2. Reduce heat and simmer for 2 minutes, then remove from heat and stir in vanilla extract.
3. Pour the mixture into molds and refrigerate for at least 2 hours until set.
4. Serve topped with diced mango.

Nutritional Facts (Per Serving): Calories: 220 | Sugars: 10g | Fat: 15g | Carbohydrates: 20g | Protein: 2g | Fiber: 3g | Sodium: 15mg

Raw Cashew Cheesecake with Blueberry Swirl

Prep: 20 minutes | Cook: 25 minutes | Serves: 8

Ingredients:

- 1 1/2 cups raw cashews, soaked overnight (210g)
- 1/4 cup coconut oil, melted (60ml)
- 1/4 cup maple syrup (60ml)
- 1/4 cup lemon juice (60ml)
- 1 tsp vanilla extract (5ml)
- 1 cup blueberries (150g)
- 1/2 cup dates, pitted (90g)
- 1/2 cup almonds (70g)
- 2 tbsp low carb sweeteners (30g)

Instructions:

1. Blend dates and almonds in a food processor until they form a sticky mixture. Press into the bottom of a springform pan.
2. In a blender, mix soaked cashews, coconut oil, maple syrup, lemon juice, and vanilla extract until smooth.
3. Pour cashew mixture over the crust.
4. Puree blueberries and swirl into the cashew mixture.
5. Freeze for at least 4 hours before serving.

Nutritional Facts (Per Serving): Calories: 220 | Sugars: 12g | Fat: 15g | Carbohydrates: 22g | Protein: 4g | Fiber: 3g | Sodium: 10mg

Raw Brownies with Walnuts

Prep: 15 minutes | Cook: 25 minutes | Serves: 8

Ingredients:

- 1 cup dates, pitted (150g)
- 1 cup walnuts (120g)
- 1/4 cup unsweetened cocoa powder (30g)
- 2 tbsp low carb sweeteners (30g)
- 1 tsp vanilla extract (5ml)
- 1/8 tsp salt (1g)

Instructions:

1. In a food processor, blend dates and walnuts until a sticky dough forms.
2. Add cocoa powder, low carb sweeteners, vanilla extract, and salt. Blend until well combined.
3. Press mixture into a parchment-lined baking dish and refrigerate for at least 1 hour.
4. Cut into squares and serve.

Nutritional Facts (Per Serving): Calories: 220 | Sugars: 16g | Fat: 12g | Carbohydrates: 28g | Protein: 4g | Fiber: 4g | Sodium: 30mg

Vegan Lemon Bars

Prep: 15 minutes | Cook: 25 minutes | Serves: 8

Ingredients:

- 1 cup almonds (140g)
- 1 cup dates, pitted (150g)
- 1 1/2 cups raw cashews, soaked overnight (210g)
- 1/4 cup coconut oil, melted (60ml)
- 1/4 cup maple syrup (60ml
- 1/4 cup lemon juice (60ml)
- 2 tbsp lemon zest (30g)
- 1 tsp vanilla extract (5ml)
- 2 tbsp low carb sweeteners (30g)

Instructions:

1. Blend almonds and dates in a food processor until they form a sticky crust. Press into the bottom of a baking dish.
2. In a blender, mix soaked cashews, coconut oil, maple syrup, lemon juice, lemon zest, vanilla extract, and low carb sweeteners until smooth.
3. Pour cashew mixture over the crust and freeze for at least 4 hours.
4. Cut into bars and serve.

Nutritional Facts (Per Serving): Calories: 220 | Sugars: 12g | Fat: 15g | Carbohydrates: 22g | Protein: 4g | Fiber: 3g | Sodium: 10mg

Coconut Almond Energy Bites

Prep: 10 minutes | Cook: 30 minutes | Serves: 9

Ingredients:

- 1 cup unsweetened shredded coconut (80g)
- 1/2 cup almond butter (120g)
- 1/4 cup maple syrup or agave nectar (60ml)
- 1/4 cup chopped almonds (40g)
- 2 tbsp chia seeds (30g)
- 1 tsp vanilla extract (5ml)
- Pinch of salt

Instructions:

1. In a mixing bowl, combine shredded coconut, almond butter, maple syrup, chopped almonds, chia seeds, vanilla extract, and a pinch of salt.
2. Mix well until the mixture is sticky and well combined.
3. Roll the mixture into small balls, about 1 inch in diameter.
4. Place the energy bites on a parchment-lined tray and refrigerate for at least 30 minutes to set.
5. Store in an airtight container in the refrigerator for up to two weeks.

Nutritional Facts (Per Serving): Calories: 220 | Sugars: 10g | Fat: 14g | Carbohydrates: 20g | Protein: 5g | Fiber: 6g | Sodium: 60mg

Vegan Chocolate Chip Blondies

Prep: 15 minutes | Cook: 20 minutes | Serves: 8

Ingredients:

- 1 cup almond flour (100g)
- 1/2 cup rolled oats (45g)
- 1/4 cup low carb sweeteners (30g)
- 1/4 cup coconut oil, melted (60ml)
- 1/4 cup almond milk (60ml)
- 1 tsp vanilla extract (5ml)
- 1/2 tsp baking powder (2g)
- 1/4 cup mini dark chocolate chips (45g)

Instructions:

1. Preheat oven to 350°F (175°C).
2. In a bowl, mix almond flour, rolled oats, low carb sweeteners, melted coconut oil, almond milk, vanilla extract, and baking powder until well combined.
3. Stir in mini dark chocolate chips.
4. Pour the mixture into a parchment-lined baking dish and bake for 20 minutes.
5. Let cool before cutting into squares.

Nutritional Facts (Per Serving): Calories: 220 | Sugars: 7g | Fat: 14g | Carbohydrates: 20g | Protein: 5g | Fiber: 3g | Sodium: 80mg

CHAPTER 15: DESSERT:
Baking for the Whole Family

Vegan Banana Bread with Walnuts

Prep: 15 minutes | Cook: 50 minutes | Serves: 8

Ingredients:

- 3 ripe bananas, mashed (360g)
- 1/4 cup coconut oil, melted (60ml)
- 1/4 cup low carb sweeteners (30g)
- 1/4 cup almond milk (60ml)
- 1 tsp vanilla extract (5ml)
- 1 1/2 cups gluten-free all-purpose flour (180g)
- 1 tsp baking soda (5g)
- 1/2 cup chopped walnuts (60g)
- 1/2 tsp salt (2.5g)

Instructions:

1. Preheat oven to 350°F (175°C).
2. Mix mashed bananas, melted coconut oil, low carb sweeteners, almond milk, and vanilla extract.
3. Add gluten-free all-purpose flour, baking soda, and salt; stir until combined.
4. Fold in chopped walnuts.
5. Pour into a greased loaf pan and bake for 50 minutes, or until a toothpick comes out clean.
6. Let cool before slicing.

Nutritional Facts (Per Serving): Calories: 220 | Sugars: 10g | Fat: 12g | Carbohydrates: 26g | Protein: 4g | Fiber: 4g | Sodium: 150mg

Vegan Oatmeal Raisin Cookies

Prep: 15 minutes | Cook: 10 minutes | Serves:12

Ingredients:

- 1/2 cup coconut oil, melted (120ml)
- 3/4 cup brown sugar or coconut sugar (150g)
- 1/4 cup unsweetened applesauce (60ml)
- 2 cups gluten-free rolled oats (180g)
- 1 tsp baking soda (5g)
- 1/2 tsp salt (2.5g)
- 1 cup raisins (150g)
- 1 tsp ground cinnamon (5g)
- 2 tsp vanilla extract (10ml)

Instructions:

1. Preheat oven to 350°F (175°C)
2. Combine melted coconut oil, brown sugar, and applesauce. Stir in vanilla extract.
3. In a separate bowl, whisk oats, baking soda, salt, and cinnamon.
4. Gradually add dry ingredients to the wet mixture until well mixed. Fold in raisins.
5. Drop tablespoon-sized dough portions onto the baking sheet, spacing 2 inches apart. Slightly flatten each cookie.
6. For 10-12 minutes until edges are golden brown.

Nutritional Facts (Per Serving): Calories: 220 | Sugars: 10g | Fat: 14g | Carbohydrates: 22g | Protein: 2g | Fiber: 2g | Sodium: 100mg

Lemon Poppy Seed Muffins

Prep: 15 minutes | Cook: 20 minutes | Serves:12

Ingredients:

- 1 1/2 cups gluten-free all-purpose flour (180g)
- 1/2 cup low carb sweeteners (100g)
- 2 tbsp poppy seeds (20g)
- 1 tsp baking powder (5g)
- 1/2 tsp baking soda (2.5g)
- 1/4 tsp salt (1.25g)
- 1 cup almond milk (240ml)
- 1/4 cup coconut oil, melted (60ml)
- 1/4 cup lemon juice (60ml)
- 1 tbsp lemon zest (6g)
- 1 tsp vanilla extract (5ml)

Instructions:

1. Preheat oven to 375°F (190°C). Line a muffin tin with paper liners.

2. In a large bowl, combine flour, low carb sweeteners, poppy seeds, baking powder, baking soda, and salt.

3. In a separate bowl, mix almond milk, melted coconut oil, lemon juice, lemon zest, and vanilla extract.

4. Add wet ingredients to dry ingredients, stirring until just combined.

5. Divide batter evenly among muffin cups and bake for 18-20 minutes, until a toothpick inserted into the center comes out clean.

6. Cool in the tin for 5 minutes.

Nutritional Facts (Per Serving): Calories: 220 | Sugars: 10g | Fat: 10g | Carbohydrates: 28g | Protein: 3g | Fiber: 2g | Sodium: 120mg

Cranberry Orange Scones

Prep: 15 minutes | Cook: 20 minutes | Serves: 8

Ingredients:

- 2 cups gluten-free all-purpose flour (240g)
- 1/4 cup low carb sweeteners (50g)
- 1 tbsp baking powder (15g)
- 1/2 tsp salt (2.5g)
- 1/2 cup coconut oil, cold and solid (120ml)
- 1/2 cup dried cranberries (60g)
- 1 tbsp orange zest (6g)
- 1/2 cup almond milk (120ml)
- 1 tsp vanilla extract (5ml)

Instructions:

1. Preheat oven to 400°F (200°C). Line a baking sheet with parchment paper.

2. In a large bowl, combine flour, low carb sweeteners, baking powder, and salt.

3. Cut in the cold coconut oil until the mixture resembles coarse crumbs.

4. Stir in dried cranberries and orange zest.

5. Add almond milk and vanilla extract, mixing until just combined.

6. Turn the dough onto a floured surface and shape into a disk about 1-inch thick. Cut into 8 wedges.

7. Place wedges on the baking sheet and bake for 18-20 minutes, until golden brown.

8. Cool on a wire rack.

Nutritional Facts (Per Serving): Calories: 220 | Sugars: 10g | Fat: 12g | Carbohydrates: 28g | Protein: 3g | Fiber: 2g | Sodium: 150mg

Ginger Molasses Cookies

Prep: 15 minutes | Cook: 10 minutes | Serves:12

Ingredients:

- 1/2 cup coconut oil, melted (120ml)
- 1/2 cup low carb sweeteners (100g)
- 1/4 cup molasses (60ml)
- 1 flax egg (1 tbsp flaxseed meal + 3 tbsp water) (15ml flaxseed meal + 45ml water)
- 2 cups gluten-free all-purpose flour (240g)
- 1 tsp baking soda (5g)
- 1/2 tsp salt (2.5g)
- 1 tsp ground ginger (5g)
- 1 tsp ground cinnamon (5g)
- 1/2 tsp ground cloves (2.5g)

Instructions:

1. Preheat oven to 350°F (175°C).
2. In a bowl, mix melted coconut oil, low carb sweeteners, molasses, and flax egg until well combined.
3. In a separate bowl, combine flour, baking soda, salt, ginger, cinnamon, and cloves. Gradually add to wet ingredients, mixing until a dough forms.
4. Roll dough into balls and place on a baking sheet. Flatten slightly.
5. Bake for 10-12 minutes, until edges are set.
6. Cool on a wire rack.

Nutritional Facts (Per Serving): Calories: 220 | Sugars: 10g | Fat: 10g | Carbohydrates: 30g | Protein: 2g | Fiber: 1g | Sodium: 120mg

Vegan Apple Pie with Cinnamon Crust

Prep: 30 minutes | Cook: 45 minutes | Serves: 8

Ingredients:

- 2 cups gluten-free all-purpose flour (240g)
- 1/2 cup coconut oil, solid (120ml)
- 1/4 cup low carb sweeteners (50g)
- 1/2 tsp salt (2.5g)
- 1/2 cup cold water (120ml)
- 6 cups sliced apples (700g)
- 1/4 cup low carb sweeteners (50g)
- 2 tbsp lemon juice (30ml)
- 1 tsp ground cinnamon (5g)
- 1/4 tsp ground nutmeg (1.25g)
- 1 tbsp cornstarch (15g)

Instructions:

1. Preheat oven to 375°F (190°C).
2. In a bowl, combine flour, low carb sweeteners, and salt. Cut in solid coconut oil until the mixture resembles coarse crumbs. Add cold water gradually, mixing until a dough forms. Divide dough in half and roll out each half to fit a pie dish.
3. In a large bowl, mix sliced apples, low carb sweeteners, lemon juice, cinnamon, nutmeg, and cornstarch until apples are evenly coated.
4. Place one rolled-out dough in the bottom of the pie dish, add apple mixture, and cover with the second rolled-out dough. Seal and flute the edges.
6. Bake for 45 minutes.

Nutritional Facts (Per Serving): Calories: 220 | Sugars: 12g | Fat: 12g | Carbohydrates: 30g | Protein: 2g | Fiber: 3g | Sodium: 150mg

Vegan Chocolate Cake with Avocado Frosting

Prep: 20 minutes | Cook: 25 minutes | Serves: 8

Ingredients:

- 1 1/2 cups gluten-free all-purpose flour (180g)
- 1 cup low carb sweeteners (200g)
- 1/3 cup unsweetened cocoa powder (40g)
- 1 tsp baking soda (5g)
- 1/2 tsp salt (2.5g)
- 1 cup water (240ml)
- 1/2 cup coconut oil, melted (120ml)
- 1 tbsp apple cider vinegar (15ml)
- 1 tsp vanilla extract (5ml)

Frosting:
- 2 ripe avocados (400g)
- 1/2 cup unsweetened cocoa powder (60g)
- 1/2 cup low carb sweeteners (100g)
- 1 tsp vanilla extract (5ml)

Instructions:

1. Preheat oven to 350°F (175°C).

2. In a large bowl, mix flour, low carb sweeteners, cocoa powder, baking soda, and salt.

3. Add water, melted coconut oil, apple cider vinegar, and vanilla extract to the dry ingredients. Mix until smooth.

4. Pour the batter into the prepared cake pan and bake for 25-30 minutes, until a toothpick inserted into the center comes out clean.

5. For the frosting, blend avocados, cocoa powder, low carb sweeteners, and vanilla extract until smooth.

Nutritional Facts (Per Serving): Calories: 220 | Sugars: 10g | Fat: 14g | Carbohydrates: 25g | Protein: 3g | Fiber: 5g | Sodium: 150mg

Vegan Snickerdoodles

Prep: 15 minutes | Cook: 10 minutes | Serves:12

Ingredients:

- 1/2 cup coconut oil, melted (120ml)
- 1/2 cup brown sugar or coconut sugar (100g)
- 1/4 cup unsweetened applesauce (60ml)
- 1 tsp baking soda (5g)
- 2 tsp ground cinnamon (10g)
- 2 cups gluten-free all-purpose flour (240g)
- 1/4 tsp salt (1g)
- 1/4 cup brown sugar or coconut sugar (50g)
- 1 tsp ground cinnamon (5g)
- 2 tsp vanilla extract (10ml)

Instructions:

1. Preheat oven to 350°F (175°C) and line a baking sheet with parchment.

2. Mix coconut oil, brown sugar, applesauce, and vanilla until smooth.

3. Combine flour, baking soda, and salt; add to wet mixture to form dough.

4. Prepare Coating: Mix ½ cup brown sugar with cinnamon.

5. Roll dough into balls, coat in cinnamon sugar, and place 2 inches apart on the sheet.

6. Bake for 10-12 minutes until edges are set.

Cool on baking sheet for 5 minutes, then transfer to a wire rack.

7. Serve or store in an airtight container.

Nutritional Facts (Per Serving): Calories: 220 | Sugars: 8g | Fat: 14g | Carbohydrates: 18g | Protein: 6g | Fiber: 3g | Sodium: 100mg

CHAPTER 16: DINNER:
Flavorful Curries and Stir-Fries

Cauliflower and Potato Curry

Prep: 20 minutes | Cook: 30 minutes | Serves: 4

Ingredients:

- 3 cups cauliflower florets (300g)
- 2 medium potatoes, diced (300g)
- 1 onion, finely chopped (150g)
- 2 cloves garlic, minced (10g)
- 1 tbsp ginger, minced (15g)
- 2 cups canned tomatoes (400g)
- 1 cup coconut milk (240ml)
- 2 tsp ground cumin (4g)
- 2 tsp ground coriander (4g)
- 1 tsp turmeric (2g)
- 1 tsp chili powder (2g)
- 1 tsp salt (6g)
- 2 tbsp vegetable oil (30ml)
- Fresh cilantro for garnish

Instructions:

1. Heat oil in a large pan over medium heat. Add onion, garlic, and ginger; sauté until soft.
2. Add cumin, coriander, turmeric, and chili powder; cook for 1 minute.
3. Stir in tomatoes and bring to a simmer.
4. Add potatoes and cauliflower; cook until tender, about 20 minutes.
5. Pour in coconut milk and salt; simmer for an additional 5 minutes.

6. Garnish with cilantro and serve.

Nutritional Facts (Per Serving): Calories: 380 | Sugars: 9g | Fat: 19g | Carbohydrates: 45g | Protein: 8g | Fiber: 10g | Sodium: 600mg

Chickpea and Pumpkin

Prep: 15 minutes | Cook: 25 minutes | Serves: 4

Ingredients:

- 1 cup chickpeas, cooked (240g)
- 2 cups pumpkin, diced (400g)
- 1 onion, finely chopped (150g)
- 2 cloves garlic, minced (10g)
- 1 tbsp ginger, minced (15g)
- 2 cups canned tomatoes (400g)
- 1 cup coconut milk (240ml)
- 2 tsp curry powder (4g)
- 1 tsp cumin seeds (2g)
- 1 tsp turmeric (2g)
- 1 tsp salt (6g)
- 2 tbsp vegetable oil (30ml)
- 2 cups wild rice, cooked (360g)
- Fresh cilantro for garnish

Instructions:

1. Heat oil in a pan and sizzle cumin seeds.
2. Sauté onion, garlic, and ginger until soft.

3. Add curry powder and turmeric; cook for 1 minute.

4. Stir in tomatoes, then add pumpkin and chickpeas; cook for 15 minutes.

5. Pour in coconut milk and salt; simmer for 5 minutes.

6. Serve over wild rice, garnished with cilantro.

Nutritional Facts (Per Serving): Calories: 380 | Sugars: 7g | Fat: 18g | Carbohydrates: 48g | Protein: 9g | Fiber: 11g | Sodium: 600mg

2. Add garlic and ginger; sauté for 1 minute.

3. Add broccoli, bell pepper, carrot, and snap peas; stir-fry until vegetables are tender-crisp.

4. Stir in teriyaki sauce and soy sauce; cook for another 2-3 minutes.

5. Serve over brown rice, garnished with sesame seeds and green onions.

Nutritional Facts (Per Serving): Calories: 380 | Sugars: 8g | Fat: 16g | Carbohydrates: 46g | Protein: 14g | Fiber: 7g | Sodium: 600mg

Sweet and Sour Vegetable Stir-Fry

Prep 15 minutes | Cook: 20 minutes | Serves: 4

Ingredients:

- 2 cups broccoli florets (300g)
- 1 red bell pepper, sliced (150g)
- 1 carrot, julienned (100g)
- 1 cup snap peas (100g)
- 1 onion, sliced (150g)
- 2 tbsp vegetable oil (30ml)
- 1/4 cup low-carb vegan sweetener (50g)
- 1/4 cup rice vinegar (60ml)
- 1/4 cup soy sauce (60ml)
- 2 tbsp vegan ketchup (30g)
- 1 tbsp cornstarch (15g)
- 2 cups jasmine rice, cooked (360g)
- Green onions for garnish

Instructions:

1. Heat oil in a large skillet over medium-high heat. Add onion, bell pepper, broccoli, carrot, and snap peas; stir-fry until tender-crisp.

2. In a bowl, mix sweetener, vinegar, soy sauce, vegan ketchup, and cornstarch. Add to skillet and cook until sauce thickens.

3. Serve stir-fry over jasmine rice, garnished with green onions.

Nutritional Facts (Per Serving): Calories: 380 | Sugars: 12g | Fat: 10g | Carbohydrates: 65g | Protein: 7g | Fiber: 6g | Sodium: 600mg

Teriyaki Tofu Stir-Fry

Prep: 15 minutes | Cook: 20 minutes | Serves: 4

Ingredients:

- 14 oz firm tofu, cubed (400g)
- 2 cups broccoli florets (300g)
- 1 red bell pepper, sliced (150g)
- 1 carrot, julienned (100g)
- 1 cup snap peas (100g)
- 1/2 cup teriyaki sauce (120ml)
- 2 tbsp soy sauce (30ml)
- 2 tbsp vegetable oil (30ml)
- 2 cloves garlic, minced (10g)
- 1 tbsp ginger, minced (15g)
- 2 cups cooked brown rice (360g)
- Sesame seeds and green onions for garnish

Instructions:

1. Heat oil in a large skillet over medium-high heat. Add tofu and cook until golden brown.

CHAPTER 17: DINNER:
Gourmet Stuffed Vegetables and Cutlets

Stuffed Bell Peppers

Prep: 15 minutes | Cook: 30 minutes | Serves: 4

Ingredients:

- 4 large bell peppers (600g)
- 1 cup quinoa, cooked (170g)
- 1 cup black beans, cooked (240g)
- 1 cup corn kernels (160g)
- 1 onion, finely chopped (150g)
- 1 tsp cumin (2g)
- 1 tsp chili powder (2g)
- 1/2 tsp salt (3g)
- 1/2 cup tomato sauce (120ml)
- 1 tbsp vegetable oil (15ml)
- Fresh cilantro for garnish
- 2 cloves garlic, minced

Instructions:

1. Preheat oven to 375°F (190°C). Cut tops off bell peppers and remove seeds.
2. Heat oil in a pan over medium heat. Sauté onion and garlic until soft. Add cumin, chili powder, and salt.
3. Stir in quinoa, black beans, corn, and tomato sauce; cook for 5 minutes.
4. Stuff bell peppers with quinoa mixture. Place in a baking dish and bake for 20-25 minutes.

Nutritional Facts (Per Serving): Calories: 380 | Sugars: 8g | Fat: 9g | Carbohydrates: 63g | Protein: 13g | Fiber: 12g | Sodium: 600mg

Mushroom and Lentil Stuffed Tomatoes

Prep: 15 minutes | Cook: 30 minutes | Serves: 4

Ingredients:

- 4 large tomatoes (600g)
- 1 cup lentils, cooked (200g)
- 1 cup mushrooms, chopped (150g)
- 1 onion, finely chopped (150g)
- 2 cloves garlic, minced (10g)
- 1 tsp thyme (2g)
- 1/2 tsp salt (3g)
- 1/2 tsp black pepper (2g)
- 1/2 cup gluten-free breadcrumbs or ground gluten-free oats (60g)
- 2 tbsp olive oil (30ml)
- Fresh parsley for garnish

Instructions:

1. Preheat oven to 375°F (190°C). Cut tops off tomatoes and scoop out the insides.
2. Heat olive oil in a pan over medium heat. Sauté onion, garlic, and mushrooms until soft.
3. Add lentils, thyme, salt, and pepper; cook for 5 minutes. Stir in gluten-free breadcrumbs or ground oats.
4. Stuff tomatoes with lentil mixture. Place in a baking dish and bake for 20-25 minutes.
5. Garnish with parsley and serve.

Nutritional Facts (Per Serving): Calories: 380 | Sugars: 9g | Fat: 14g | Carbohydrates: 51g | Protein: 13g | Fiber: 12g | Sodium: 600mg

Stuffed Cabbage Rolls

Prep: 20 minutes | Cook: 45 minutes | Serves: 4

Ingredients:

- 8 large cabbage leaves (400g)
- 1 cup cooked rice (180g)
- 1 cup cooked lentils (200g)
- 1 onion, finely chopped (150g)
- 2 cloves garlic, minced (10g)
- 2 tbsp tomato paste (30g)
- 1 tsp thyme (2g)
- 1/2 tsp salt (3g)
- 1/2 tsp black pepper (2g)
- 2 cups tomato sauce (480ml)
- 2 tbsp olive oil (30ml)

Instructions:

1. Preheat oven to 375°F (190°C). Blanch cabbage leaves in boiling water for 2-3 minutes until pliable.
2. In a pan, heat olive oil over medium heat. Sauté onion and garlic until soft.
3. Mix in rice, lentils, tomato paste, thyme, salt, and pepper.
4. Place 2 tbsp of filling on each cabbage leaf, roll, and place in a baking dish.
5. Pour tomato sauce over rolls and bake for 30 minutes.

Nutritional Facts (Per Serving): Calories: 380 | Sugars: 9g | Fat: 11g | Carbohydrates: 58g | Protein: 13g | Fiber: 11g | Sodium: 600mg

Mushroom and Walnut Stuffed Squash

Prep: 15 minutes | Cook: 45 minutes | Serves: 4

Ingredients:

- 2 medium acorn squash, halved and seeded (800g)
- 1 cup mushrooms, chopped (150g)
- 1 cup walnuts, chopped (120g)
- 1 onion, finely chopped (150g)
- 2 cloves garlic, minced (10g)
- 1 tsp thyme (2g)
- 1/2 tsp salt (3g)
- 1/2 tsp black pepper (2g)
- 2 tbsp olive oil (30ml)
- Fresh parsley for garnish

Instructions:

1. Preheat oven to 375°F (190°C). Place squash halves cut side down on a baking sheet and bake for 30 minutes.
2. In a pan, heat olive oil over medium heat. Sauté onion, garlic, and mushrooms until soft.
3. Stir in walnuts, thyme, salt, and pepper. Cook for 5 minutes.
4. Fill squash halves with mushroom mixture and bake for an additional 15 minutes.
5. Garnish with parsley and serve.

Nutritional Facts (Per Serving): Calories: 380 | Sugars: 6g | Fat: 24g | Carbohydrates: 38g | Protein: 8g | Fiber: 8g | Sodium: 400mg

Stuffed Sweet Potatoes with Chickpeas and Tahini

Prep: 10 minutes | Cook: 40 minutes | Serves: 4

Ingredients:

- 4 medium sweet potatoes (800g)
- 1 cup cooked chickpeas (240g)
- 2 tbsp tahini (30g)
- 1 tbsp lemon juice (15ml)
- 2 cloves garlic, minced (10g)
- 1 tsp cumin (2g)
- 1/2 tsp salt (3g)
- 1/4 cup water (60ml)
- 2 tbsp olive oil (30ml)
- Fresh parsley for garnish

Instructions:

1. Preheat oven to 400°F (200°C). Bake sweet potatoes for 35-40 minutes until tender.
2. In a bowl, mix chickpeas, tahini, lemon juice, garlic, cumin, salt, and water until combined.
3. Cut sweet potatoes in half and fill with chickpea mixture.
4. Drizzle with olive oil and garnish with parsley before serving.

Nutritional Facts (Per Serving): Calories: 380 | Sugars: 12g | Fat: 13g | Carbohydrates: 58g | Protein: 9g | Fiber: 11g | Sodium: 450mg

Zucchini Boats

Prep: 15 minutes | Cook: 25 minutes | Serves: 4

Ingredients:

- 4 medium zucchinis, halved lengthwise (600g)
- 1 cup cooked chickpeas (240g)
- 1 cup diced tomatoes (200g)
- 1 onion, finely chopped (150g)
- 2 cloves garlic, minced (10g)
- 1 tsp cumin (2g)
- 1 tsp paprika (2g)
- 1/2 tsp salt (3g)
- 1/4 tsp cayenne pepper (1g)
- 2 tbsp olive oil (30ml)
- Fresh parsley for garnish

Instructions:

1. Preheat oven to 375°F (190°C). Scoop out the centers of the zucchini halves.
2. Heat olive oil in a pan over medium heat. Sauté onion and garlic until soft.
3. Add chickpeas, tomatoes, cumin, paprika, salt, and cayenne; cook for 5 minutes.
4. Stuff zucchini halves with the chickpea mixture. Place in a baking dish and bake for 20 minutes.
5. Garnish with parsley and serve.

Nutritional Facts (Per Serving): Calories: 380 | Sugars: 10g | Fat: 14g | Carbohydrates: 56g | Protein: 9g | Fiber: 14g | Sodium: 600mg

CHAPTER 18: DINNER:
Creative and Colorful Salads

Mediterranean Chickpea Salad

Prep: 15 minutes | Serves: 4

Ingredients:

- 2 cups cooked chickpeas (480g)
- 1 cucumber, diced (150g)
- 2 tomatoes, diced (300g)
- 1/2 cup olives, sliced (75g)
- 1/4 cup red onion, finely chopped (40g)
- 1/4 cup lemon juice (60ml)
- 2 tbsp olive oil (30ml)
- 1 tsp dried oregano (2g)
- 1/2 tsp salt (3g)
- 1/4 tsp black pepper (1g)
- Fresh parsley for garnish

Instructions:

1. In a large bowl, combine chickpeas, cucumber, tomatoes, olives, and red onion.
2. In a small bowl, whisk together lemon juice, olive oil, oregano, salt, and black pepper.
3. Pour the dressing over the salad and toss to combine.
4. Garnish with parsley and serve.

Nutritional Facts (Per Serving): Calories: 380 | Sugars: 7g | Fat: 14g | Carbohydrates: 52g | Protein: 11g | Fiber: 13g | Sodium: 600mg

Southwest Black Bean Salad

Prep: 15 minutes | Serves: 4

Ingredients:

- 2 cups cooked black beans (480g)
- 1 cup corn kernels (160g)
- 1 avocado, diced (200g)
- 1 red bell pepper, diced (150g)
- 1/4 cup red onion, finely chopped (40g)
- 1/4 cup cilantro, chopped (10g)
- 1/4 cup lime juice (60ml)
- 2 tbsp olive oil (30ml)
- 1 tsp cumin (2g)
- 1/2 tsp salt (3g)
- 1/4 tsp black pepper (1g)

Instructions:

1. In a large bowl, combine black beans, corn, avocado, bell pepper, red onion, and cilantro.
2. In a small bowl, whisk together lime juice, olive oil, cumin, salt, and black pepper.
3. Pour the dressing over the salad and toss to combine.
4. Serve immediately.

Nutritional Facts (Per Serving): Calories: 380 | Sugars: 4g | Fat: 17g | Carbohydrates: 48g | Protein: 10g | Fiber: 16g | Sodium: 500mg

Asian Sesame Noodle Salad

Prep: 15 minutes | Cook: 10 minutes | Serves: 4

Ingredients:

- 8 oz rice noodles (240g)
- 1 cup shredded carrots (100g)
- 1 cup sliced bell peppers (150g)
- 1 cup sliced cucumber (150g)
- 1/4 cup chopped green onions (30g)
- 1/4 cup sesame seeds (35g)
- 1/4 cup gluten-free tamari or coconut aminos (60ml)
- 2 tbsp sesame oil (30ml)
- 2 tbsp rice vinegar (30ml)
- 1 tbsp low carb sweetener (15g)
- 1 tbsp grated ginger (15g)
- 1 clove garlic, minced (5g)

Instructions:

1. Cook noodles according to package instructions. Rinse with cold water and drain.
2. In a large bowl, combine noodles, carrots, bell peppers, cucumber, and green onions.
3. In a small bowl, whisk together gluten-free tamari or coconut aminos, sesame oil, rice vinegar, sweetener, ginger, and garlic.
4. Pour dressing over salad, toss to combine, and sprinkle with sesame seeds.

Nutritional Facts (Per Serving): Calories: 380 | Sugars: 5g | Fat: 12g | Carbohydrates: 58g | Protein: 7g | Fiber: 5g | Sodium: 600mg

Mexican Quinoa Salad

Prep: 15 minutes | Cook: 15 minutes | Serves: 4

Ingredients:

- 1 cup quinoa, cooked (185g)
- 1 cup black beans, cooked (240g)
- 1 cup corn kernels (160g)
- 1 avocado, diced (200g)
- 1 red bell pepper, diced (150g)
- 1/4 cup red onion, finely chopped (40g)
- 1/4 cup chopped cilantro (10g)
- 1/4 cup lime juice (60ml)
- 2 tbsp olive oil (30ml)
- 1 tsp cumin (2g)
- 1/2 tsp salt (3g)
- 1/4 tsp black pepper (1g)

Instructions:

1. In a large bowl, combine quinoa, black beans, corn, avocado, bell pepper, red onion, and cilantro.
2. In a small bowl, whisk together lime juice, olive oil, cumin, salt, and black pepper.
3. Pour dressing over salad and toss to combine.

Nutritional Facts (Per Serving): Calories: 380 | Sugars: 5g | Fat: 17g | Carbohydrates: 48g | Protein: 9g | Fiber: 12g | Sodium: 400mg

Rainbow Quinoa Salad

Prep: 15 minutes | Cook: 15 minutes | Serves: 4

Ingredients:

- 1 cup quinoa, cooked (185g)
- 1/2 cup cherry tomatoes, halved (75g)
- 1/2 cup diced cucumber (75g)
- 1/2 cup shredded carrots (50g)
- 1/2 cup diced red bell pepper (75g)
- 1/4 cup chopped red onion (40g)
- 1/4 cup chopped parsley (10g)
- 1/4 cup lemon juice (60ml)
- 2 tbsp tahini (30g)
- 2 tbsp olive oil (30ml)
- 1 tsp low carb sweetener (5g)
- 1/2 tsp salt (3g)
- 1/4 tsp black pepper (1g)

Instructions:

1. In a large bowl, combine quinoa, cherry tomatoes, cucumber, carrots, bell pepper, red onion, and parsley.
2. In a small bowl, whisk together lemon juice, tahini, olive oil, sweetener, salt, and black pepper.
3. Pour dressing over salad and toss to combine.

Nutritional Facts (Per Serving): Calories: 380 | Sugars: 6g | Fat: 17g | Carbohydrates: 48g | Protein: 9g | Fiber: 8g | Sodium: 400mg

Zucchini and Tomato Salad

Prep: 15 minutes | Serves: 4

Ingredients:

- 4 medium zucchinis, spiralized (600g)
- 2 cups cherry tomatoes, halved (300g)
- 1/4 cup fresh basil, chopped (10g)
- 2 tbsp olive oil (30ml)
- 1/4 cup balsamic vinegar (60ml)
- 1 tsp low carb sweetener (5g)
- 1/2 tsp salt (3g)
- 1/4 tsp black pepper (1g)

Instructions:

1. In a large bowl, combine spiralized zucchini, cherry tomatoes, and basil.
2. In a small bowl, whisk together balsamic vinegar, olive oil, sweetener, salt, and black pepper.
3. Pour dressing over salad and toss to combine.
4. Serve immediately.

Nutritional Facts (Per Serving): Calories: 380 | Sugars: 10g | Fat: 18g | Carbohydrates: 50g | Protein: 5g | Fiber: 7g | Sodium: 400mg

CHAPTER 19: DINNER: Family-Style Dinner Ideas

Mushroom Stroganoff

Prep: 10 minutes | Cook: 20 minutes | Serves: 4

Ingredients:

- 1 lb mushrooms, sliced (450g)
- 1 onion, finely chopped (150g)
- 2 cloves garlic, minced (10g)
- 1 cup vegetable broth (240ml)
- 1 cup unsweetened almond milk (240ml)
- 2 tbsp gluten-free all-purpose flour (15g)
- 2 tbsp olive oil (30ml)
- 1 tbsp soy sauce (15ml)
- 1 tsp paprika (2g)
- 1/2 tsp salt (3g)
- 1/4 tsp black pepper (1g)
- 8 oz gluten-free noodles, cooked (225g)
- Fresh parsley for garnish

Instructions:

1. Heat olive oil in a large pan over medium heat. Sauté onion and garlic until soft.
2. Add mushrooms and cook until they release their juices.
3. Stir in gluten-free flour, cooking for 1 minute. Add vegetable broth, almond milk, gluten-free tamari or coconut aminos, paprika, salt, and black pepper.
4. Simmer until sauce thickens, about 10 minutes.
5. Serve over cooked gluten-free noodles and garnish with parsley.

Nutritional Facts (Per Serving): Calories: 380 | Sugars: 5g | Fat: 14g | Carbohydrates: 53g | Protein: 11g | Fiber: 8g | Sodium: 600mg

Eggplant Parmesan

Prep: 20 minutes | Cook: 30 minutes | Serves: 4

Ingredients:

- 2 large eggplants, sliced (800g)
- 2 cups marinara sauce (480ml)
- 1 cup vegan cheese, shredded (120g)
- 1 cup gluten-free breadcrumbs (120g)
- 1/2 cup gluten-free all-purpose flour (60g)
- 2 tbsp ground flaxseed mixed with 6 tbsp water (30g flaxseed, 90ml water)
- 2 tbsp olive oil (30ml)
- 1 tsp dried oregano (2g)
- 1/2 tsp salt (3g)
- 1/4 tsp black pepper (1g)

Instructions:

1. Preheat oven to 375°F (190°C). Line a baking sheet with parchment paper.
2. Dip eggplant slices in flour, then flaxseed mixture, then breadcrumbs mixed with oregano, salt, and pepper.

3. Place on baking sheet and drizzle with olive oil. Bake for 20 minutes until golden.

4. In a baking dish, layer baked eggplant slices, marinara sauce, and vegan cheese. Repeat layers.

5. Bake for another 10 minutes until cheese melts.

Nutritional Facts (Per Serving): Calories: 380 | Sugars: 10g | Fat: 15g | Carbohydrates: 53g | Protein: 8g | Fiber: 12g | Sodium: 600mg

4. Fill each tortilla with the bean mixture, roll, and place seam side down in the dish.

5. Pour remaining enchilada sauce over the top. Bake for 20 minutes.

6. Garnish with cilantro and serve.

Nutritional Facts (Per Serving): Calories: 380 | Sugars: 8g | Fat: 14g | Carbohydrates: 56g | Protein: 10g | Fiber: 12g | Sodium: 600mg

Vegan Enchiladas

Prep: 20 minutes | Cook: 25 minutes | Serves: 4

Ingredients:

- 8 gluten-free corn tortillas (200g)
- 1 can black beans, drained and rinsed (15 oz / 425g)
- 1 cup corn kernels (160g)
- 1 bell pepper, diced (150g)
- 1 onion, finely chopped (150g)
- 2 cloves garlic, minced (10g)
- 2 cups gluten-free enchilada sauce (480ml)
- 1 tsp cumin (2g)
- 1 tsp chili powder (2g)
- 2 tbsp olive oil (30ml)
- Fresh cilantro for garnish

Instructions:

1. Preheat oven to 375°F (190°C). Heat olive oil in a pan over medium heat. Sauté onion and garlic until soft.

2. Add bell pepper, black beans, corn, cumin, and chili powder; cook for 5 minutes.

3. Spread 1/2 cup enchilada sauce on the bottom of a baking dish.

Margherita Pizza with Cashew Mozzarella

Prep: 20 minutes | Cook: 15 minutes | Serves: 4

Ingredients:

- 1 gluten-free pizza crust (250g)
- 1 cup tomato sauce (240ml)
- 2 cups cherry tomatoes, halved (300g)
- 1/2 cup fresh basil leaves (20g)
- 1 cup raw cashews, soaked (150g)
- 1/4 cup water (60ml)
- 2 tbsp lemon juice (30ml)
- 2 tbsp nutritional yeast (14g)
- 1 tbsp olive oil (15ml)
- 1 clove garlic (5g)
- 1/2 tsp salt (3g)

Instructions:

1. Preheat oven to 450°F (230°C). Prepare pizza crust on a baking sheet.

2. In a blender, combine soaked cashews, water, lemon juice, nutritional yeast, olive oil, garlic, and salt; blend until smooth.

3. Spread tomato sauce over pizza crust. Add dollops of cashew mozzarella and cherry tomatoes.
4. Bake for 12-15 minutes until crust is golden.
5. Garnish with fresh basil leaves before serving.

Nutritional Facts (Per Serving): Calories: 380 | Sugars: 7g | Fat: 18g | Carbohydrates: 45g | Protein: 10g | Fiber: 6g | Sodium: 600mg

Mushroom and Spinach White Pizza with Garlic Sauce

Prep: 20 minutes | Cook: 15 minutes | Serves: 4

Ingredients:

- 1 gluten-free pizza crust (250g)
- 1 cup sliced mushrooms (150g)
- 2 cups fresh spinach (60g)
- 1/2 onion, thinly sliced (75g)
- 2 cloves garlic, minced (10g)
- 2 tbsp gluten-free all-purpose flour (15g)
- 2 tbsp olive oil (30ml)
- 1/2 cup vegan mozzarella, shredded (60g)
- 1/2 tsp salt (3g)
- 1/4 tsp black pepper (1g)
- 1 cup unsweetened almond milk (240ml)

Instructions:

1. Preheat oven to 450°F (230°C) and prepare pizza crust. Sauté mushrooms, spinach, and onion in olive oil until soft.
2. Make garlic sauce by whisking flour and garlic in olive oil, then gradually add almond milk until thickened. Season with salt and pepper.
4. Spread sauce on crust, top with veggies and vegan mozzarella.
5. Bake for 12-15 minutes until crust is golden.

Nutritional Facts (Per Serving): Calories: 380 | Sugars: 5g | Fat: 16g | Carbohydrates: 48g | Protein: 10g | Fiber: 6g | Sodium: 600mg

Roasted Vegetable and Pesto Pizza

Prep: 15 minutes | Cook: 20 minutes | Serves: 4

Ingredients:

- 1 gluten-free pizza crust (250g)
- 1 cup cherry tomatoes, halved (150g)
- 1 zucchini, sliced (150g)
- 1 red bell pepper, sliced (150g)
- 1/2 cup red onion, sliced (75g)
- 1/4 cup gluten-free pesto (60g)
- 1 cup vegan mozzarella, shredded (120g)
- 2 tbsp olive oil (30ml)
- Salt and pepper to taste

Instructions:

1. Preheat oven to 450°F (230°C). Arrange vegetables on a baking sheet, drizzle with olive oil, and season with salt and pepper. Roast for 15 minutes.
2. Spread pesto over pizza crust. Add roasted vegetables and sprinkle with vegan mozzarella.
3. Bake for 10-12 minutes until crust is golden.

Nutritional Facts (Per Serving): Calories: 380 | Sugars: 7g | Fat: 18g | Carbohydrates: 45g | Protein: 9g | Fiber: 5g | Sodium: 600mg

CHAPTER 20: DINNER: Holiday Specialties

Vegan Wellington

Prep: 25 minutes | Cook: 40 minutes | Serves: 4

Ingredients:

- 1 sheet gluten-free puff pastry (250g)
- 2 cups mushrooms, chopped (300g)
- 1 cup cooked lentils (200g)
- 1 onion, finely chopped (150g)
- 2 cloves garlic, minced (10g)
- 2 tbsp olive oil (30ml)
- 1 tbsp soy sauce (15ml)
- 1 tsp thyme (2g)
- 1/2 tsp salt (3g)
- 1/4 tsp black pepper (1g)
- 1/4 cup gluten-free breadcrumbs (30g)

Instructions:

1. Preheat oven to 375°F (190°C). Heat olive oil in a pan over medium heat. Sauté onion, garlic, and mushrooms until soft.
2. Add lentils, soy sauce, thyme, salt, and pepper. Cook for 5 minutes. Stir in breadcrumbs.
3. Roll out puff pastry on a baking sheet. Place mushroom mixture in the center and fold pastry over, sealing the edges.
4. Bake for 35-40 minutes until golden brown.

Nutritional Facts (Per Serving): Calories: 380 | Sugars: 3g | Fat: 21g | Carbohydrates: 40g | Protein: 10g | Fiber: 5g | Sodium: 600mg

Butternut Squash and Apple Casserole

Prep: 15 minutes | Cook: 45 minutes | Serves: 4

Ingredients:

- 4 cups butternut squash, cubed (600g)
- 2 apples, peeled and sliced (300g)
- 1/2 cup certified gluten-free rolled oats (50g)
- 1/4 cup low carb sweetener (50g)
- 2 tbsp almond flour (15g)
- 2 tbsp coconut oil, melted (30ml)
- 1 tsp cinnamon (2g)
- 1/4 tsp nutmeg (1g)
- 1/4 tsp salt (1g)

Instructions:

1. Preheat oven to 350°F (175°C). In a baking dish, combine butternut squash and apples.
2. In a bowl, mix oats, sweetener, almond flour, coconut oil, cinnamon, nutmeg, and salt. Sprinkle over squash and apples.
3. Bake for 45 minutes until squash is tender and topping is golden.

Nutritional Facts (Per Serving): Calories: 380 | Sugars: 16g | Fat: 14g | Carbohydrates: 60g | Protein: 3g | Fiber: 10g | Sodium: 150mg

Stuffed Acorn Squash with Quinoa and Cranberries

Prep: 20 minutes | Cook: 40 minutes | Serves: 4

Ingredients:

- 2 medium acorn squashes, halved and seeded (800g)
- 1 cup cooked quinoa (185g)
- 1/2 cup dried cranberries (60g)
- 1/4 cup chopped pecans (30g)
- 1/4 cup chopped parsley (10g)
- 1/4 cup orange juice (60ml)
- 2 tbsp olive oil (30ml)
- 1 tbsp maple syrup (15ml)
- 1/2 tsp salt (3g)
- 1/4 tsp black pepper (1g)

Instructions:

1. Preheat oven to 375°F (190°C). Place squash halves cut side down on a baking sheet. Roast for 30 minutes.

2. In a bowl, mix cooked quinoa, cranberries, pecans, parsley, orange juice, olive oil, maple syrup, salt, and pepper.

3. Fill roasted squash halves with quinoa mixture. Bake for another 10 minutes.

Nutritional Facts (Per Serving): Calories: 380 | Sugars: 19g | Fat: 14g | Carbohydrates: 63g |

Protein: 6g | Fiber: 8g | Sodium: 300mg

Lentil Loaf

Prep: 20 minutes | Cook: 1 hour | Serves: 6

Ingredients:

- 1 1/2 cups cooked lentils (250g)
- 1 cup finely chopped carrots (120g)
- 1 cup finely chopped celery (120g)
- 1 cup finely chopped onion (150g)
- 2 cloves garlic, minced
- 1 cup certified gluten-free rolled oats (90g)
- 1/2 cup gluten-free breadcrumbs (60g)
- 1/4 cup low carb sweetener (50g)
- 1/4 cup ketchup (60ml)
- 2 tbsp gluten-free tamari or coconut aminos (30ml)
- 2 Tbsp olive oil (30ml)
- 1 tsp thyme (5g)
- 1 tsp rosemary (5g)
- Salt and pepper to taste

Instructions:

1. Preheat oven to 350°F (175°C).

2. In a large bowl, combine cooked lentils, carrots, celery, onion, and garlic.

3. Stir in gluten-free rolled oats, gluten-free breadcrumbs, sweetener, ketchup, gluten-free tamari or coconut aminos, olive oil, thyme, rosemary, salt, and pepper.

4. Transfer the mixture to the prepared loaf pan and press down firmly.

5. Bake for 1 hour, until the top is golden brown and firm to the touch.

6. Let cool in the pan for 10 minutes before slicing and serving with mashed potatoes and gravy.

Nutritional Facts (Per Serving): Calories: 380 | Sugars: 6g | Fat: 8g | Carbohydrates: 55g | Protein: 12g | Fiber: 15g | Sodium: 600mg

Roasted Vegetable Platter

Prep: 15 minutes | Cook: 30 minutes | Serves: 4

Ingredients:

- 1 red bell pepper, sliced (150g)
- 1 yellow bell pepper, sliced (150g)
- 1 zucchini, sliced (150g)
- 1 eggplant, cubed (200g)
- 1 red onion, sliced (150g)
- 2 tbsp olive oil (30ml)
- 2 tbsp balsamic glaze (30ml)
- 1 tsp salt (5g)
- 1/2 tsp black pepper (2g)
- 1 tsp dried thyme (2g)

Instructions:

1. Preheat oven to 400°F (200°C). Arrange vegetables on a baking sheet.
2. Drizzle with olive oil, sprinkle with salt, pepper, and thyme. Toss to coat.
3. Roast for 25-30 minutes until tender and slightly charred.
4. Drizzle with balsamic glaze before serving.

Nutritional Facts (Per Serving): Calories: 380 | Sugars: 12g | Fat: 15g | Carbohydrates: 57g | Protein: 5g | Fiber: 10g | Sodium: 600mg

Avocado and Cherry Tomato Pizza with Basil

Prep: 15 minutes | Cook: 15 minutes | Serves: 4

Ingredients:

- 1 pizza crust (250g)
- 2 ripe avocados, sliced (300g)
- 1 cup cherry tomatoes, halved (150g)
- 1/4 cup fresh basil leaves, chopped (10g)
- 1 cup vegan mozzarella, shredded (120g)
- 2 tbsp olive oil (30ml)
- 1 tbsp lemon juice (15ml)
- 1/2 tsp salt (3g)
- 1/4 tsp black pepper (1g)

Instructions:

1. Preheat oven to 450°F (230°C). Prepare pizza crust on a baking sheet.
2. Brush crust with olive oil and bake for 5 minutes.
3. Top with vegan mozzarella and cherry tomatoes. Bake for another 8-10 minutes until cheese is melted.
4. In a bowl, toss avocado slices with lemon juice, salt, and pepper.
5. Top pizza with avocado and fresh basil before serving.

Nutritional Facts (Per Serving): Calories: 380 | Sugars: 5g | Fat: 23g | Carbohydrates: 38g | Protein: 6g | Fiber: 8g | Sodium: 600mg

CHAPTER 21: BONUSES

Personalized 30-Day Vegan Shopping Plan for One

Embark on a delightful vegan culinary adventure with our meticulously crafted 30-day grocery shopping guide, specifically designed for individual needs. As envisioned by a professional vegan chef, this guide streamlines your meal preparation by focusing on fresh, whole plant-based ingredients and reducing reliance on processed foods. Pay close attention to concealed sugars, particularly in store-bought sauces and dressings, to maintain the integrity of your natural flavors. Customize the quantities to fit your personal requirements, ensuring you adhere to the vegan principles of simplicity and wholesomeness.

Shopping List for 7-Day Meal Plan

Vegetables:

- **Avocados** – 4 large / 800g (*Coconut Yogurt Parfait, Quinoa and Black Bean Salad with Avocado, Black Bean Breakfast Burrito, Avocado Chocolate Mousse*)
- **Cauliflower** – 2 medium heads / 900g (*Cauliflower and Potato Curry, Curried Cauliflower and Chickpea Stew*)
- **Potatoes** – 4 large / 600g (*Cauliflower and Potato Curry, Sweet Potato Hash*)
- **Sweet Potatoes** – 3 large / 900g (*Sweet Potato Hash, Sweet Potato Shepherd's Pie*)
- **Onions** – 6 medium / 900g
- **Garlic** – 2 bulbs / 30g
- **Spinach** – 8 cups / 240g (*Veggie-Packed Omelette, Chickpea and Spinach Pilaf, Spinach and Mushroom Quiche, Spiced Chickpea and Spinach Stew, Spinach and Artichoke Risotto, Spinach and Mushroom Lasagna*)
- **Red Bell Peppers** – 4 medium / 600g (*Quinoa and Black Bean Salad with Avocado, Black Bean Breakfast Burrito, Stuffed Bell Peppers, Zucchini and Corn Pita*)
- **Mushrooms** – 4 cups / 600g (*Mushroom Stroganoff, Creamy Spinach and Mushroom Pasta, Eggplant Parmesan, Mushroom and Spinach White Pizza with Garlic Sauce*)
- **Eggplant** – 2 large / 600g (*Eggplant Parmesan, Eggplant and Tomato Shakshuka*)
- **Zucchini** – 3 medium / 450g (*Zucchini and Corn Pita, Stuffed Zucchini Boats*)
- **Carrots** – 5 medium / 500g (*Sweet Potato Hash, Hearty Vegetable and Lentil Stew, Butternut Squash and Chickpea Soup*)
- **Celery Stalks** – 2 stalks / 200g (*Spaghetti with Lentil Bolognese*)
- **Asparagus** – 1 bunch / 200g (*Lemon Asparagus Risotto*)
- **Butternut Squash** – 2 medium / 800g (*Butternut Squash and Chickpea Soup, Butternut Squash and Sage Risotto*)
- **Artichoke Hearts** – 1 can / 400g (*Spinach and Artichoke Risotto*)

Fruits:

- **Blueberries** – 1 pint / 300g (*Blueberry Almond Bars, Blueberry Millet Porridge*)
- **Bananas** – 4 medium / 400g (*Walnut and Banana Breakfast Bowl, Pancakes with Almond Butter and Bananas*)
- **Mangoes** – 2 large / 600g (*Coconut Milk Panna Cotta with Mango*)
- **Pomegranates** – 1 / 200g (*Quinoa Breakfast Bowl*)
- **Limes** – 4 / 240g (*Quinoa and Black Bean Salad with Avocado, Sweet and Sour Vegetable Stir-Fry*)
- **Lemons** – 3 / 150g (*Vegan Lemon Bars, Lemon Asparagus Risotto*)
- **Cherries** – 1 cup / 150g (*Cherry Cashew Bars*)
- **Figs** – 6 dried / 180g (*Fig and Hazelnut Bars*)
- **Apples** – 3 medium / 600g (*Vegan Lemon Bars*)

Grains & Bread:

- **Quinoa** – 4 cups / 720g (*Quinoa and Black Bean Salad with Avocado, Quinoa Breakfast Bowl, Butternut Squash and Quinoa Stew*)
- **Brown Rice** – 2 cups / 360g (*Broccoli and Rice Casserole*)
- **Orzo** – 1 cup / 180g (*Creamy Tomato Basil Soup with Orzo*)
- **Gluten-Free Pitas** – 6 pitas / 720g (*Hummus and Veggie Pita, Zucchini and Corn Pita*)
- **Gluten-Free Tortillas** – 4 / 400g (*Black Bean Breakfast Burrito, Black Bean Burger with Avocado*)
- **Gluten-Free Lasagna Noodles** – 8 sheets / 960g (*Spinach and Mushroom Lasagna*)
- **Gluten-Free Pasta** – 2 lbs / 900g (*Creamy Spinach and Mushroom Pasta, Avocado Basil Pesto Pasta, Spaghetti with Lentil Bolognese*)

Dairy Alternatives:

- **Coconut Yogurt** – 2 cups / 480g (*Coconut Yogurt Parfait*)
- **Plant-Based Milk (Almond,**

Soy, or Oat) – 4 cups / 960ml (*Various Recipes*)
- **Vegan Parmesan or Nutritional Yeast** – 1 cup / 240g (*Various Recipes*)
- **Vegan Cheese (Cashew Mozzarella)** – 2 cups / 480g (*Margherita Pizza with Cashew Mozzarella*)

Nuts, Seeds & Nut Butters:

- **Raw Cashews** – 3 cups / 450g (*Creamy Spinach and Mushroom Pasta, Raw Brownies with Walnuts, Vegan Snickerdoodles*)
- **Walnuts** – 2 cups / 300g (*Walnut and Banana Breakfast Bowl, Raw Brownies with Walnuts*)
- **Almonds** – 1 cup / 150g (*Blueberry Almond Bars*)
- **Chia Seeds** – 1/2 cup / 75g (*Chia Seed Pudding*)
- **Flaxseeds** – 1/4 cup / 30g (*Black Bean Breakfast Burrito*)
- **Pumpkin Seeds** – 1/2 cup / 75g (*Various Recipes*)

Pantry Staples:

- **Olive Oil** – 2 bottles / 1 liter each (*Various Recipes*)
- **Coconut Oil** – 1 jar / 500g (*Various Recipes*)
- **Maple Syrup** – 1 bottle / 500ml (*Various Recipes*)
- **Gluten-Free Breadcrumbs or Ground Gluten-Free Oats** – 2 cups / 240g (*Red Lentil and Quinoa Patties, Black Bean Burger with Avocado*)
- **Tomato Paste** – 1 can / 120g (*Various Recipes*)
- **Canned Black Beans** – 3 cans / 900g
- **Canned Chickpeas** – 3 cans / 900g
- **Canned Lentils** – 2 cans / 600g (*Hearty Vegetable and Lentil Stew*)
- **Canned Diced Tomatoes** – 4 cans / 1600g (*Various Recipes*)
- **Canned Artichoke Hearts** – 1 can / 400g (*Spinach and Artichoke Risotto*)
- **Gluten-Free Flour Blends** – 2 cups / 240g (*Pumpkin Protein Pancakes, Vegan Snickerdoodles*)
- **Baking Powder** – 1 small container / 50g
- **Spices (Cumin, Paprika, Turmeric, Cinnamon, Nutmeg, Salt, Pepper)** – 1 each

Refrigerated Items:

- **Firm Tofu** – 2 blocks / 800g total (*Spiced Chickpea and Spinach Stew, Stuffed Zucchini Boats*)
- **Plant-Based Yogurt** – 2 cups / 480g (*Coconut Yogurt Parfait*)

Frozen Items:

- **Frozen Peas** – 2 bags / 600g (Various Recipes)

Shopping List for 8-14 Day Meal Plan

Vegetables:

- **Avocados** – 3 large / 600g (*Walnut and Banana Breakfast Bowl, Quinoa and Black Bean Salad with Avocado, Stuffed Sweet Potatoes with Chickpeas and Tahini*)
- **Zucchini** – 4 medium / 600g (*Zucchini and White Bean Stew, Zucchini and Corn Pita, Stuffed Zucchini Boats*)
- **Cauliflower** – 2 medium heads / 900g (*Cauliflower and Potato Curry*)
- **Potatoes** – 3 large / 450g (*Cauliflower and Potato Curry*)
- **Sweet Potatoes** – 4 large / 1200g (*Chickpea and Pumpkin, Stuffed Sweet Potatoes with Chickpeas and Tahini*)
- **Onions** – 4 medium / 600g
- **Garlic** – 2 bulbs / 30g
- **Spinach** – 6 cups / 180g (*Chickpea and Spinach Pilaf, Chickpea and Spinach Pilaf, Stuffed Cabbage Rolls*)
- **Red Bell Peppers** – 2 medium / 300g (*Stuffed Cabbage Rolls*)
- **Mushrooms** – 2 cups / 300g (*Stuffed Cabbage Rolls*)
- **Eggplant** – 1 large / 300g (*Smoky Eggplant and Tomato Stew*)
- **Carrots** – 2 medium / 200g (*Zucchini and White Bean Stew*)
- **Celery Stalks** – 1 stalk / 100g (*Red Lentil and Quinoa Patties*)
- **Asparagus** – 1/2 bunch / 100g (*Sweet and Sour Vegetable Stir-Fry*)
- **Butternut Squash** – 1 medium / 400g (*Butternut Squash and Quinoa Stew*)
- **Artichoke Hearts** – 0.5 can / 200g (*Sun-Dried Tomato and Basil Hummus with Pita Chips*)

Fruits:

- **Blueberries** – 0.5 pint / 150g (*Cherry Almond Quinoa*)
- **Bananas** – 2 medium / 200g (*Walnut and Banana Breakfast Bowl*)
- **Mangoes** – 1 large / 300g (*Coconut Almond Energy Bites*)
- **Pomegranates** – 0.5 / 100g (*Pomegranate Quinoa*)
- **Limes** – 2 / 120g (*Jalapeño Lime Hummus with Rice Crackers*)
- **Lemons** – 1 / 50g (*Vegan Snickerdoodles*)
- **Cherries** – 0.5 cup / 75g (*Cherry Almond Quinoa*)
- **Figs** – 3 dried / 90g (*Fig and Almond Oats*)
- **Apples** – 1.5 medium / 300g (*Avocado and Cilantro Hummus with Veggie Sticks*)

Grains & Bread:

- **Quinoa** – 3 cups / 540g (*Quinoa and Black Bean Salad with Avocado, Pomegranate Quinoa*)
- **Brown Rice** – 1 cup / 180g (*Chickpea and Spinach Pilaf*)
- **Orzo** – 0.5 cup / 90g (*Quinoa and Black Bean Salad with Avocado*)
- **Gluten-Free Pitas** – 3 pitas / 360g (*Sun-Dried Tomato and Basil Hummus with Pita Chips*)
- **Gluten-Free Tortillas** – 2 / 200g (*Vegan Snickerdoodles*)
- **Gluten-Free Lasagna Noodles** – 4 sheets / 480g (*Stuffed*

Cabbage Rolls)
- **Gluten-Free Pasta** – 1 lb / 450g (*Teriyaki Tofu Stir-Fry*)

Dairy Alternatives:

- **Coconut Yogurt** – 1 cup / 240g (*Coconut Almond Energy Bites*)
- **Plant-Based Milk (Almond, Soy, or Oat)** – 2 cups / 480ml (*Various Recipes*)
- **Vegan Parmesan or Nutritional Yeast** – 0.5 cup / 120g (*Vegan Snickerdoodles*)
- **Vegan Cheese (Cashew Mozzarella)** – 1 cup / 240g (*Roasted Vegetable and Pesto Pizza*)

Nuts, Seeds & Nut Butters:

- **Raw Cashews** – 1.5 cups / 225g (*Chickpea and Pumpkin*)
- **Walnuts** – 1 cup / 150g (*Walnut and Banana Breakfast Bowl*)
- **Almonds** – 0.5 cup / 75g (*Cherry Almond Quinoa*)
- **Chia Seeds** – 0.25 cup / 37g (*Chickpea and Pumpkin*)
- **Flaxseeds** – 0.125 cup / 15g (*Chickpea and Pumpkin*)
- **Pumpkin Seeds** – 0.25 cup / 37g (*Chickpea and Pumpkin*)

Pantry Staples:

- **Olive Oil** – 1 bottle / 500ml (*Various Recipes*)
- **Coconut Oil** – 0.5 jar / 250g (*Various Recipes*)
- **Maple Syrup** – 250ml (*Various Recipes*)
- **Gluten-Free Breadcrumbs or Ground Gluten-Free Oats** – 1 cup / 120g (*Red Lentil and Quinoa Patties*)
- **Tomato Paste** – 0.5 can / 60g (*Vegan Snickerdoodles*)
- **Vegetable Broth** – 2 quarts / 1.9 liters (*Various Recipes*)
- **Canned Black Beans** – 1.5 cans / 450g (*Quinoa and Black Bean Salad with Avocado*)
- **Canned Chickpeas** – 1.5 cans / 450g (*Chickpea and Pumpkin*)
- **Canned Lentils** – 1 can / 300g (*Red Lentil and Quinoa Patties*)
- **Canned Diced Tomatoes** – 2

cans / 800g (*Various Recipes*)
- **Canned Artichoke Hearts** – 0.5 can / 200g (*Sun-Dried Tomato and Basil Hummus with Pita Chips*)
- **Gluten-Free Flour Blends** – 1 cup / 120g (*Vegan Snickerdoodles*)
- **Baking Powder** – 0.5 small container / 25g (*Vegan Snickerdoodles*)
- **Spices (Cumin, Paprika, Turmeric, Cinnamon, Nutmeg, Salt, Pepper)** – 1 each
- **Vegan Sweeteners (Agave, Maple Syrup)** – 1 bottle / 500ml (*Various Recipes*)
- **Vanilla Extract** – 1 bottle / 60ml

Refrigerated Items:

- **Firm Tofu** – 1 block / 400g total (*Teriyaki Tofu Stir-Fry*)
- **Plant-Based Yogurt** – 1 cup / 240g (*Avocado and Cilantro Hummus with Veggie Sticks*)

Frozen Items:

- **Frozen Peas** – 1 bag / 300g (*Sweet and Sour Vegetable Stir-Fry*)

Shopping List for 15-21 Day Meal Plan

Vegetables:

- **Avocados** – 3 large / 600g (*Walnut and Banana Breakfast Bowl, Stuffed Sweet Potatoes with Chickpeas and Tahini*)
- **Zucchini** – 4 medium / 600g (*Zucchini and White Bean Stew, Zucchini and Corn Pita, Stuffed Zucchini Boats*)
- **Cauliflower** – 2 medium heads / 900g (*Cauliflower and Potato Curry*)
- **Potatoes** – 3 large / 600g (*Cauliflower and Potato Curry, Cauliflower and Potato Curry*)
- **Sweet Potatoes** – 4 large / 1200g (*Sweet Potato Hash, Sweet Potato Shepherd's Pie, Stuffed Sweet Potatoes with*

Chickpeas and Tahini)
- **Onions** – 8 medium / 1200g
- **Garlic** – 3 bulbs / 45g
- **Spinach** – 10 cups / 300g (*Chickpea and Spinach Pilaf, Spinach and Artichoke Risotto, Spinach and Mushroom Quiche, Spiced Chickpea and Spinach Stew*)
- **Red Bell Peppers** – 6 medium / 900g (*Stuffed Bell Peppers, Stuffed Cabbage Rolls*)
- **Mushrooms** – 6 cups / 900g (*Mushroom and Walnut Stuffed Squash, Mushroom Stroganoff, Creamy Spinach and Mushroom Pasta, Stuffed Cabbage Rolls*)
- **Eggplant** – 2 large / 600g (*Smoky Eggplant Baba Ganoush with Whole Wheat Pita, Smoky Eggplant and Tomato Stew*)
- **Carrots** – 4 medium / 400g (*Sweet Potato Hash, Zucchini and White Bean Stew*)
- **Celery Stalks** – 1 stalk / 100g (*Spaghetti with Lentil Bolognese*)
- **Asparagus** – 1 bunch / 200g (*Lemon Asparagus Risotto*)
- **Butternut Squash** – 1 medium / 400g (*Butternut Squash and Quinoa Stew, Butternut Squash and Sage Risotto*)
- **Artichoke Hearts** – 1 can / 400g (*Spinach and Artichoke Risotto*)
- **Mini Bell Peppers** – 6 / 300g (*Mini Bell Peppers Stuffed with Guacamole*)
- **Portobello Mushrooms** – 4 large / 600g (*Stuffed Portobello Mushrooms*)
- **Tomatoes** – 6 medium / 600g (*Stuffed Cabbage Rolls, Mushroom and Lentil Stuffed Tomatoes*)
- **Cucumbers** – 2 medium / 300g (*Pumpkin and Sage Hummus with Cucumber Slices*)

Fruits:

- **Blueberries** – 1 pint / 300g (*Blueberry Almond Bars, Blueberry Millet Porridge*)
- **Bananas** – 4 medium / 400g (*Pancakes with Almond Butter*

and Bananas)

- **Mangoes** – 1 large / 300g (*Coconut Almond Energy Bites*)
- **Pomegranates** – 1 / 200g (*Pomegranate Quinoa*)
- **Limes** – 2 / 120g (*Jalapeño Lime Hummus with Rice Crackers*)
- **Lemons** – 1 / 50g (*Vegan Snickerdoodles*)
- **Cherries** – 1/2 cup / 75g (*Cherry Almond Quinoa*)
- **Figs** – 3 dried / 90g (*Fig and Almond Oats*)
- **Apples** – 1.5 medium / 300g (*Avocado and Cilantro Hummus with Veggie Sticks*)

Grains & Bread:

- **Quinoa** – 3 cups / 540g (*Quinoa and Black Bean Salad with Avocado, Pomegranate Quinoa*)
- **Brown Rice** – 1 cup / 180g (*Millet and Vegetable Bowl*)
- **Orzo** – 0.5 cup / 90g (*Quinoa and Black Bean Salad with Avocado*)
- **Gluten-Free Pitas** – 3 pitas / 360g (*Smoky Eggplant Baba Ganoush with Whole Wheat Pita*)
- **Gluten-Free Tortillas** – 2 / 200g (*Sweet Potato and Black Bean Tacos*)
- **Gluten-Free Lasagna Noodles** – 4 sheets / 480g (*Stuffed Cabbage Rolls*)
- **Gluten-Free Pasta** – 1 lb / 450g (*Avocado Basil Pesto Pasta, Teriyaki Tofu Stir-Fry*)

Dairy Alternatives:

- **Coconut Yogurt** – 1 cup / 240g (*Coconut Almond Energy Bites*)
- **Plant-Based Milk (Almond, Soy, or Oat)** – 2 cups / 480ml (*Various Recipes*)
- **Vegan Parmesan or Nutritional Yeast** – 0.5 cup / 120g (*Vegan Snickerdoodles*)
- **Vegan Cheese (Cashew Mozzarella)** – 1 cup / 240g (*Roasted Vegetable and Pesto Pizza*)

Nuts, Seeds & Nut Butters:

- **Raw Cashews** – 1.5 cups / 225g (*Pumpkin and Sage Hummus with Cucumber Slices, Chickpea and Pumpkin*)
- **Walnuts** – 1 cup / 150g (*Maple Walnut Oatmeal, Mushroom and Walnut Stuffed Squash*)
- **Almonds** – 0.5 cup / 75g (*Cherry Almond Quinoa*)
- **Chia Seeds** – 0.25 cup / 37g (*Pumpkin and Sage Hummus with Cucumber Slices*)
- **Flaxseeds** – 0.125 cup / 15g (*Pumpkin and Sage Hummus with Cucumber Slices*)
- **Pumpkin Seeds** – 0.25 cup / 37g (*Pumpkin and Sage Hummus with Cucumber Slices*)

Pantry Staples:

- **Olive Oil** – 1 bottle / 500ml (*Various Recipes*)
- **Coconut Oil** – 0.5 jar / 250g (*Various Recipes*)
- **Maple Syrup** – 250ml (*Maple Walnut Oatmeal*)
- **Gluten-Free Breadcrumbs or Ground Gluten-Free Oats** – 1 cup / 120g (*Red Lentil and Quinoa Patties*)
- **Tomato Paste** – 0.5 can / 60g (*Vegan Snickerdoodles*)
- **Canned Black Beans** – 1.5 cans / 450g (*Quinoa and Black Bean Salad with Avocado*)
- **Canned Chickpeas** – 1.5 cans / 450g (*Chickpea and Pumpkin*)
- **Canned Lentils** – 1 can / 300g (*Red Lentil and Quinoa Patties*)
- **Canned Diced Tomatoes** – 2 cans / 800g (*Various Recipes*)
- **Canned Artichoke Hearts** – 0.5 can / 200g (*Sun-Dried Tomato and Basil Hummus with Pita Chips*)
- **Gluten-Free Flour Blends** – 1 cup / 120g (*Vegan Snickerdoodles*)
- **Baking Powder** – 0.5 small container / 25g (*Vegan Snickerdoodles*)
- **Spices (Cumin, Paprika, Turmeric, Cinnamon, Nutmeg, Salt, Pepper)** – 1 each

- **Vegan Sweeteners (Agave, Maple Syrup)** – 1 bottle / 500ml
- **Vanilla Extract** – 1 bottle / 60ml

Refrigerated Items:

- **Firm Tofu** – 1 block / 400g total (*Teriyaki Tofu Stir-Fry*)
- **Plant-Based Yogurt** – 1 cup / 240g (*Avocado and Cilantro Hummus with Veggie Sticks*)

Frozen Items:

- **Frozen Peas** – 1 bag / 300g (*Sweet and Sour Vegetable Stir-Fry*)

Shopping List for 22-28 Day Meal Plan

Vegetables:

- **Eggplant** – 3 large / 900g (*Eggplant and Tomato Shakshuka, Smoky Eggplant Baba Ganoush with Whole Wheat Pita, Eggplant Parmesan*)
- **Tomatoes** – 6 medium / 600g (*Eggplant and Tomato Shakshuka, Mushroom and Lentil Stuffed Tomatoes, Eggplant Parmesan*)
- **Sweet Potatoes** – 4 large / 1200g (*Sweet Potato Shepherd's Pie, Stuffed Sweet Potatoes with Chickpeas and Tahini*)
- **Chickpeas** – 2 cans / 600g (*Avocado and Cilantro Hummus with Veggie Sticks, Cumin-Spiced Falafel, Chickpea and Pumpkin, Stuffed Sweet Potatoes with Chickpeas and Tahini*)
- **Black Beans** – 1 can / 450g (*Black Bean Burger with Avocado*)
- **Mushrooms** – 6 cups / 900g (*Mushroom Stroganoff, Stuffed Bell Peppers, Portobello Mushroom Burger, Eggplant Parmesan*)
- **Red Bell Peppers** – 6 medium / 900g (*Stuffed Bell Peppers,*

Stuffed Cabbage Rolls)
- **Zucchini** – 4 medium / 600g (*Zucchini and White Bean Stew, Stuffed Zucchini Boats*)
- **Broccoli** – 2 heads / 400g (*Broccoli and Rice Casserole, Sweet and Sour Vegetable Stir-Fry*)
- **Carrots** – 4 medium / 400g (*Sweet Potato Shepherd's Pie, Zucchini and White Bean Stew*)
- **Onions** – 8 medium / 1200g
- **Garlic** – 3 bulbs / 45g
- **Spinach** – 10 cups / 300g (*Blueberry Spinach Smoothie, Spinach and Mushroom Lasagna, Spinach and Artichoke Risotto*)
- **Mini Bell Peppers** – 6 / 300g (*Mini Bell Peppers Stuffed with Guacamole*)
- **Portobello Mushrooms** – 4 large / 600g (*Portobello Mushroom Burger*)
- **Cucumbers** – 3 medium / 300g (*Pumpkin and Sage Hummus with Cucumber Slices, Cucumber Mint Smoothie*)
- **Asparagus** – 1 bunch / 200g (*Lemon Asparagus Risotto*)
- **Butternut Squash** – 1 medium / 400g (*Butternut Squash and Sage Risotto*)
- **Celery Stalks** – 1 stalk / 100g (*Spaghetti with Lentil Bolognese*)
- **Artichoke Hearts** – 1 can / 400g (*Spinach and Artichoke Risotto*)

Fruits:

- **Blueberries** – 1 pint / 300g (*Blueberry Almond Bars, Blueberry Millet Porridge*)
- **Bananas** – 4 medium / 400g (*Pancakes with Almond Butter and Bananas*)
- **Mangoes** – 1 large / 300g (*Coconut Almond Energy Bites*)
- **Pomegranates** – 1 / 200g (*Pomegranate Quinoa*)
- **Limes** – 2 / 120g (*Jalapeño Lime Hummus with Rice Crackers*)
- **Lemons** – 1 / 50g (*Vegan Snickerdoodles*)
- **Cherries** – 1/2 cup / 75g (*Cherry Almond Quinoa*)

- **Figs** – 3 dried / 90g (*Fig and Almond Oats*)
- **Apples** – 1.5 medium / 300g (*Avocado and Cilantro Hummus with Veggie Sticks*)
- **Strawberries** – 2 cups / 300g (*Strawberry Basil Smoothie*)

Grains & Bread:

- **Quinoa** – 2 cups / 360g (*Hearty Vegetable and Quinoa Soup, Pomegranate Quinoa*)
- **Brown Rice** – 1 cup / 180g (*Broccoli and Rice Casserole*)
- **Orzo** – 0.5 cup / 90g (*Hearty Vegetable and Quinoa Soup*)
- **Gluten-Free Pitas** – 4 pitas / 480g (*Hummus and Veggie Pita, Smoky Eggplant Baba Ganoush with Whole Wheat Pita*)
- **Gluten-Free Tortillas** – 6 / 600g (*Black Bean Burger with Avocado, Sweet Potato and Black Bean Tacos, Vegan Enchiladas*)
- **Gluten-Free Lasagna Noodles** – 8 sheets / 960g (*Spinach and Mushroom Lasagna*)
- **Gluten-Free Pasta** – 2 lbs / 900g (*Teriyaki Tofu Stir-Fry, Mushroom Stroganoff, Eggplant Parmesan*)

Dairy Alternatives:

- **Coconut Yogurt** – 1 cup / 240g (*Avocado and Cilantro Hummus with Veggie Sticks*)
- **Plant-Based Milk (Almond, Soy, or Oat)** – 4 cups / 960ml (*Blueberry Spinach Smoothie, Cinnamon Apple Waffles, Strawberry Basil Smoothie*)
- **Vegan Parmesan or Nutritional Yeast** – 1 cup / 240g (*Vegan Snickerdoodles*)
- **Vegan Cheese (Cashew Mozzarella)** – 2 cups / 480g (*Vegan Enchiladas, Roasted Vegetable and Pesto Pizza*)

Nuts, Seeds & Nut Butters:

- **Raw Cashews** – 1.5 cups / 225g (*Pumpkin and Sage Hummus with Cucumber Slices, Chickpea and Pumpkin*)

- **Walnuts** – 1 cup / 150g (*Maple Walnut Oatmeal, Mushroom and Walnut Stuffed Squash*)
- **Almonds** – 1/2 cup / 75g (*Cherry Almond Quinoa*)
- **Chia Seeds** – 0.25 cup / 37g (*Pumpkin and Sage Hummus with Cucumber Slices*)
- **Flaxseeds** – 0.125 cup / 15g (*Pumpkin and Sage Hummus with Cucumber Slices*)
- **Pumpkin Seeds** – 0.25 cup / 37g (*Pumpkin and Sage Hummus with Cucumber Slices*)

Pantry Staples:

- **Olive Oil** – 1 bottle / 500ml (*Various Recipes*)
- **Coconut Oil** – 0.5 jar / 250g (*Various Recipes*)
- **Maple Syrup** – 250ml (*Maple Walnut Oatmeal*)
- **Gluten-Free Breadcrumbs or Ground Gluten-Free Oats** – 1 cup / 120g (*Red Lentil and Quinoa Patties*)
- **Tomato Paste** – 0.5 can / 60g (*Vegan Snickerdoodles*)
- **Vegetable Broth** – 2 quarts / 1.9 liters (*Various Recipes*)
- **Canned Black Beans** – 1 can / 450g (*Black Bean Burger with Avocado*)
- **Canned Chickpeas** – 2 cans / 600g (*Avocado and Cilantro Hummus with Veggie Sticks, Cumin-Spiced Falafel, Chickpea and Pumpkin, Stuffed Sweet Potatoes with Chickpeas and Tahini*)
- **Canned Lentils** – 1 can / 300g (*Eggplant and Lentil Moussaka*)
- **Canned Diced Tomatoes** – 2 cans / 800g (*Eggplant and Tomato Shakshuka, Eggplant and Lentil Moussaka*)
- **Canned Artichoke Hearts** – 1 can / 400g (*Spinach and Artichoke Risotto*)
- **Gluten-Free Flour Blends** – 1 cup / 120g (*Vegan Snickerdoodles*)
- **Baking Powder** – 0.5 small container / 25g (*Vegan Snickerdoodles*)
- **Spices (Cumin, Paprika, Turmeric, Cinnamon,**

Nutmeg, Salt, Pepper) – 1 each
- **Vegan Sweeteners (Agave, Maple Syrup)** – 1 bottle / 500ml
- **Vanilla Extract** – 1 bottle / 60ml

Refrigerated Items:

- **Firm Tofu** – 1 block / 400g (*Teriyaki Tofu Stir-Fry*)
- **Plant-Based Yogurt** – 1 cup / 240g (*Avocado and Cilantro Hummus with Veggie Sticks*)

Frozen Items:

- **Frozen Peas** – 1 bag / 300g (*Sweet and Sour Vegetable Stir-Fry*)

Made in the USA
Las Vegas, NV
07 January 2025

16051351R00046